barcode = 3 8 8 8 8 2 2 0 9 1 2 8 4 9

W9-AUV-599

University Library
GOVERNORS STATE UNIVERISTY

JUN 1 5 1983

GOVERNORS STATE UNIVERSITY LIBRARY

3 1611 00174 4116

GUSTAV MAHLER

and

GUIDO ADLER

UNIVERSITY LIBRARY
GOVERNORS STATE UNIVERSITY
PARK FOREST SOUTH, ILL.

UNIVERSITY LIBRARY

GOVERNORS STATE UNIVERSITY

PARK FOREST SOUTH, ILL.

GUSTAV MAHLER AND GUIDO ADLER

RECORDS OF A FRIENDSHIP

Edward R. Reilly

UNIVERSITY LIBRARY
GOVERNORS STATE UNIVERSITY
PARK FOREST SOUTH, ILL.

CAMBRIDGE UNIVERSITY PRESS

Cambridge

London   New York   New Rochelle

Melbourne   Sydney

Published by the Press Syndicate of the University of Cambridge
The Pitt Building, Trumpington Street, Cambridge CB2 1RP
32 East 57th Street, New York, NY 10022, USA
296 Beaconsfield Parade, Middle Park, Melbourne 3206, Australia

English translation and new editorial material
© Cambridge University Press 1982

Pages 13-73 originally published in German as *Gustav Mahler* by Universal
Edition, Vienna and Leipzig 1916.
First published in English by Cambridge University Press 1982 as *Gustav Mahler*

Printed in Great Britain at the University Press, Cambridge

Library of Congress catalogue card number: 81-10262

British Library Cataloguing in publication data
Reilly, Edward R.
Gustav Mahler and Guido Adler.
1. Mahler, Gustav   2. Adler, Guido
3. Composers – Austria
4. Musicologists – Austria
I. Title
780'.92'4   ML410. M23
ISBN 0 521 23592 8

ML
410
M23
R35
1982
c.1

Not to hate, but to love, to advise, to help is the duty of the musical scholar. Art and art scholarship are not separate spheres between which the dividing lines are sharply drawn; only the nature of their treatment differs and changes according to the times. The more intimate the contact between scholarship and forward-moving art and living artists, the closer it comes to its goal: through the understanding of art to work for art.

Guido Adler, *Music and Musicology* (1898)

CONTENTS

ACKNOWLEDGMENTS

I am grateful to the editor of *The Musical Quarterly* for permission to publish the present form of my study of Mahler and Adler here; to Mrs Anna Mahler and the University of Georgia Libraries for permission to reproduce the documents at the University of Georgia; and to Mr Lawrence Schoenberg for permission to quote brief passages from unpublished letters of Arnold Schoenberg. I would also like to acknowledge the generous help that was extended to me by the following individuals and libraries: Dr Theophil Antonicek, Dr Kurt Blaukopf, Mr Jack Diether, Dr Charles Douglas, Dr Egbert Ennulat, Baron Henry-Louis de La Grange, Miss E. B. Heemskerk, Dr Ernst Hilmar, Dr Rosemary Hilmar, the late Mrs Christa Landon, Mr Knud Martner, Dr Margaret McKenzie, Dr Donald Mitchell, Mrs Ursula Richter, Mr Peter Riethus, Mr Albi Rosenthal, Dr Carl A. Rosenthal, Mr Philip Winters, The Pierpont Morgan Library, New York, The Library of Congress, Washington, DC, the Österreichische Nationalbibliothek, Vienna, the Wiener Stadtbibliothek and the Archiv der Gesellschaft der Musikfreunde in Wien. Very special thanks must go to Dr Herta Singer-Blaukopf, who, in the course of her preparation of a German edition of my study, was able to provide more accurate readings of several of the documents and offer helpful suggestions and corrections in other areas. Since the original texts of all of the manuscript sources are easily available in the German edition, they are not duplicated here. I am very grateful to Mrs Rosemary Dooley and Miss Nicola Baxter of Cambridge University Press for their interest in this study and for their help in preparing it for publication. Most of all, I am indebted to my wife, Evangeline; without her help and support, this volume would never have seen the light of day.

THE COMPOSER AND
THE MUSIC HISTORIAN

AN INTRODUCTION

Edward R. Reilly

The friendship between Gustav Mahler and Guido Adler offers a
refreshing example of the mutually beneficial interaction that can
exist between a composer and a music historian in spite of some
natural but nonetheless basic differences in outlook and perspective. The relationship between the two men is explored in this
volume from two complementary views. Adler's own well-known
study, a classic of the early Mahler literature, presents a vivid and
highly compressed summing-up of the composer's character and
achievements. My supplementary essay traces through surviving
letters and documents the course of their friendship, which
endured for more than thirty years.

These two views reflect the differing character of older and
more recent studies of Mahler. In his own time Mahler won his
share of successes as a performer and composer, but his activity in
both spheres was highly controversial. His attitudes sometimes
aroused deep animosities, and his powerful position as Director of
the Vienna Court Opera from 1897 to 1907 invited attacks that
were not infrequently intensified by anti-Semitism. Thus the
earlier books about Mahler, notably those of Paul Stefan (first
edition published in 1910),[1] Richard Specht (1913) and to a lesser
extent Adler (1914), often have a somewhat polemical cast. All
were concerned with making Mahler's creative goals clear to the
public at large, and only secondarily with presenting biographical
detail or the complex particulars surrounding the composition of
a specific work. Their researches, although undertaken with care,
made no pretense at exhaustiveness. Mahler's own sometimes
ambiguous and inaccurate statements about his works, his life and
his beliefs were generally taken at face value. Many personal
overtones and undertones also resulted from direct experiences
with Mahler and his music.

In 1920, after the hiatus created by the First World War, the
struggle for a wider acceptance of the composer's works resumed

1

with Willem Mengelberg's great Mahler festival in Amsterdam. During the period between the two wars, a handful of major new volumes appeared on Mahler. The most important were Paul Bekker's study of the symphonies (1921), Natalie Bauer-Lechner's reminiscences of the composer (published posthumously in an abridged form in 1923), Alma Mahler's edition of her husband's letters (1924) and Bruno Walter's sensitive fusion of personal and musical portraits (1936). Finally, after a new tide of anti-Jewish persecution had ended performances of Mahler's works in his homeland, Alma Mahler's *Gustav Mahler: Erinnerungen und Briefe* (1940) appeared in Holland. With this remarkable volume, the earlier body of literature about Mahler, largely the work of people who knew him directly, was essentially completed.

After the Second World War a gradual change took place in the attitudes of both the general public (especially its younger members) and a significant number of professional musicians. Performances of Mahler's works slowly grew in frequency, then burgeoned rapidly in the 1960s. By the end of that decade virtually all of the symphonies had entered the standard repertoire, and no fewer than four conductors had undertaken to record the entire cycle (now another generation has already begun to follow in their footsteps). In one of those intriguing reversals of taste that occasionally crop up in the history of music, Mahler had suddenly become a popular composer.

Coinciding with, and partly anticipating, this new acceptance, the literature about Mahler began to change in character. Inspired by their own responses to his music and by the dedicated work of earlier advocates, many younger musicians from all parts of Europe and America who grew up during the Second World War and in the years that immediately followed had become convinced that Mahler was a major composer, in spite of the strictures of some of their elders. The need to defend his musical position receded. The resulting shift in perspective was perhaps first clearly apparent in Donald Mitchell's *Gustav Mahler, The Early Years*, published in 1958. Recognizing the merits of previous studies, Mitchell explored the compositions in greater depth and raised questions about the contradictions found in published material. His approach pointed to the need for a full-scale reexamination of sources and a new search for documents of all types. The appearance of the first volume of the complete edition of Mahler's works in 1962 also drew attention to a wide variety of problems associated with the manuscripts and editions of the music. And during the 1960s an astonishing variety of documents began to reappear. Numerous unpublished letters were discovered; the forgotten 'Blumine' movement of the First Symphony was found, performed and published; the deleted first part of the cantata *Das klagende Lied* was made accessible; the libretto of the early opera *Rübezahl* was located and studied; the 'sketches' for the Tenth Symphony were shown to be a complete working draft that could be effectively realized.

In more recent years the fruits of new detailed biographical and musical research have appeared in a wealth of specialized articles and books, notably the long-awaited first volume of the large-scale work of Henry-Louis de La Grange (1973); the biography by Kurt Blaukopf (1969); and the *Mahler: A Documentary Study* (1976) of the same author, which provides a valuable and well-chosen cross-section of older, and more recently located, materials connected with the composer. With regard to the music itself, Donald Mitchell's *Gustav Mahler, The Wunderhorn Years* (1975) and the two-volume study by Constantin Floros (1977) offer both new information and new perspectives from which Mahler's works may be viewed. The 1979 colloquium devoted to Mahler in Vienna, the papers from which are soon to be published; the accompanying June issue of *Österreichische Musikzeitschrift;* and the superb exhibition mounted in Düsseldorf that same year, with an outstanding catalogue by Rudolf Stephan, may be seen as representative of the most recent, very lively, activity associated with the composer. And much further work is planned or in progress. Quite literally, hundreds of letters await publication and many facets of Mahler's life are receiving renewed scrutiny. In connection with the music, a catalogue of the composer's autographs, as well as a thematic catalogue with details of the various published texts, is in preparation, and more specific attention is already being given to various aspects of the compositions themselves in such works as Colin Matthews' doctoral thesis 'Mahler at Work' (1977), the study of the Ninth Symphony by Peter Andraschke (1976) and Norman Del Mar's work on the Sixth Symphony (1980).

This accumulation of new information about Mahler has produced what may at first seem a curious reaction. It has sharpened our appreciation of his early advocates and confirmed in many respects the perceptiveness of their basic portraits. They did not always have reliable factual information at their disposal but they grasped and conveyed essential matters with remarkable understanding. Additional research has provided a mass of new, often fascinating, detail and has clarified many specific matters. But this detail adds surprisingly little to one's fundamental conception of the man and his music.

Guido Adler has drawn a sharply-etched picture of Mahler's character as reflected in his work as a composer and conductor. Although this view is inevitably somewhat partisan, it does not gloss over some of the less attractive sides of its subject. Most importantly, it is founded on an understanding of the practical idealism that permeated so much of Mahler's work. The result is a much less overtly subjective portrait of the composer than might be expected. Recognizing the emotional intensity of Mahler's character, Adler did not underestimate his friend's conscious awareness of his actions, his skill as a strategist (note the constant military analogies) or his humor. Recognizing likewise the associative backgrounds of Mahler's compositions, Adler also understood that they justified themselves first and foremost as music, not as philosophical disquisitions.

Adler's view of Mahler has much in common with that of both Paul Stefan and Richard Specht. They all perceived his profound idealism, his struggles to achieve the highest artistic goals regardless of the personal cost and his sense of the contradictory aspects of humanity united in an all-encompassing divine whole. They also saw the enormous impact that Mahler had on Viennese musical life through his standards as a performer, the freshness of his re-creations of familiar scores and his openness to the new musical styles then emerging.

Yet there are subtle differences in Adler's perspective. He was an older man who had seen the full course of Mahler's career from his student days until his death and as a close friend knew the differences between the private and the public individual. Although he neatly countered some of the most frequent criticisms of Mahler and his works, he tended to avoid open polemics. His personal contacts with Mahler also permitted him to underline a few points unknown to other writers. But as a trained music historian, Adler kept his own personality in the background and

concentrated on the achievements of his subject as a composer
and performer. His assessments of both areas have proved
remarkably durable and his work is still an excellent introduction
to Mahler.

One encounters a real contrast when one compares this view
with that of other contemporaries, such as Ferdinand Pfohl,
whose impressions and reminiscences of Mahler's years in
Hamburg were uncovered a few years ago by Knud Martner.
While Pfohl's work is ostensibly an attempt to counteract a
supposed canonization of Mahler by Schoenberg, the author
actually goes much further. He pictures Mahler as a man who
lacked true creative ability, whose works were the result of sheer
will and his determination to *make* himself a composer. Moreover, while Mahler's skills are sporadically acknowledged or
praised, Pfohl's anecdotes are designed to suggest a naive boor
who was not above sacrificing his friends and his beliefs to his
ambitions. In Pfohl, who had been originally a sympathetic
supporter of Mahler, one senses the bitterness of a man who feels
that he has been used and whose views in later years are tinged
with anti-Semitism. But however little credence one may give to
certain of the basic implications of this oddly obtuse account of
Mahler, one must recognize that its views are quite representative
of those of a considerable number of the composer's contemporaries. Indeed Pfohl's opinions are mild in comparison with those
expressed in some of the Viennese newspapers of Mahler's day.
But it was to attitudes such as these that Guido Adler, Paul Stefan
and Richard Specht addressed themselves.

The present translation of Adler's essay - the first in English - is
the offshoot of the study of the relationship between the composer
and the historian that constitutes the second half of this volume.
The core of this study is the group of documents connected with
Mahler found among Adler's papers in the Library of the University of Georgia. These include letters of Mahler, his wife and
others who played a part in his career; all of Adler's occasional
pieces connected with the composer, as well as a variety of miscel-
laneous documents; and the original manuscript of Adler's essay
together with some of the notes accumulated in the course of its
preparation. Although these sources are meager for certain
periods in the friendship between Mahler and Adler, they clarify a
number of aspects of the relationship and provide solid evidence

of the help that Adler gave Mahler at several critical points in his life. They also confirm the antagonism between Adler and Alma Mahler during the years immediately preceding and following the composer's death. In this connection Mahler's biographers have begun only recently to approach Frau Mahler's description of her husband's activities and friendships with some caution. She knew, for example, but failed to mention, that Mahler could have remained in Vienna in a different post after he left the Court Opera in 1907. Adler, on the other hand, had been actively involved in arranging this position for Mahler, and saw his wife's demands for material comforts as the basis of the composer's decision to undertake the remunerative but exhausting series of visits to the United States. One must also be wary of this view, but knowledge of the fact that Mahler could have continued to work in Vienna draws attention once more to his conscious choice between alternatives. His love for Alma, I believe, was unquestionably the dominating factor of the last years of his life, and he *chose* to risk his own life for her.

Mahler's letters to Adler suggest the easy familiarity that existed between them and put some of the differences in their views and opinions in a clearer perspective. Since both Natalie Bauer-Lechner and Alma Mahler reported several instances in which Mahler expressed his irritation with Adler, the latter's own diffidence in writing of his personal associations with the composer left him in an anomalous position. Any serious investigation of Adler's own personality and work will reveal that he was far from the conservative fuddy-duddy suggested by Alma Mahler, but elements of this interpretation still seem to persist without the questioning that they deserve.

Mahler and Adler certainly disagreed about a number of matters, but their differences were natural elements within a genuine friendship and must be seen in this context and not as detached anecdotes. Adler was a professional music historian and his rationalistic concern for method and system in his approach to the history of music found little response in Mahler's creative and intuitive character; but, as paradoxical as it may seem, it is this very concern that underlies the growth in imaginative understanding of a wider range of music from the past and present that has developed in this century. As broad as Mahler's musical sympathies were, ranging from his childhood love of folk and military music through his mature knowledge of the works of his contemporaries, some natural limits are apparent. His devotion to Bach is well known and firmly documented. But, like many of his contemporaries, he seems to have had little feeling for, or understanding of, the composers of the earlier Baroque, Renaissance and Medieval periods (although one does find occasionally parallels in his music with some stylistic features of these periods). Adler's interests extended from non-Western cultures through all of the periods of Western music, and his methodology encouraged an awareness of the distinctive features of different earlier and more modern styles that has enormously broadened the range of music accessible to modern audiences and helped to extend our ability to understand idioms other than those of the late Baroque, Classic and Romantic eras in their own terms.

Mahler's view of the history of music, judging from the all-too-limited material available,[2] still seems to have been bound to some extent by evolutionary notions that equated a growth in expression and the means of expression with a growth in the complexity of musical language and the need to communicate with ever-growing masses of people. Yet, when in a letter of 1893 he raises the critical question, 'But then, was Bach inferior to Beethoven, or Wagner?', he begs off with the suggestion that his correspondent 'had better contact someone who can, in one glance, give you an over-all impression of the whole spiritual history of humanity'.[3] Perhaps additional material will be located eventually that will shed more light on how Mahler might have resolved this crucial issue. At present it appears that he was, quite naturally, too preoccupied with the music of his own time and with those traditions that formed its immediate foundations (from Bach forward) to explore more remote musical territory. The bond between Mahler and Adler rested not on any shared view of music's past, but on a common youthful background, equal devotion to music as one of the finest manifestations of the human spirit and a shared love of many of the great composers within the eighteenth- and nineteenth-century Austrian and German traditions, especially Mozart, Beethoven and Wagner.

Since Adler's name may be unfamiliar to the general reader today, it is useful to recall that in his own time he was a well-known and influential figure in Viennese musical life. For more than fifty years he was a leader in the field of European musicology. He is cited most frequently as the founder and general editor of the Denkmäler der Tonkunst in Österreich (Monuments of Music in Austria), a pioneer historical series devoted to the publication of major works connected with the history of music in Austria. But this occupation was only one facet of a wide variety of activities that included the writing of books and articles on an extraordinarily broad range of topics; a teaching career that made the Musikhistorisches Institut of the University of Vienna one of the major centers of European musical research; and public pursuits that drew attention to Austria's musical heritage, especially through festivals commemorating its major composers.

Adler's efforts in the direction of developing more systematic ('scientific') foundations for the study of his field as a whole resulted in two books, *Der Stil in der Musik* (1911) and *Methode der Musikgeschichte* (1919), in which he sought to identify and categorize the different areas that form essential components of musical research. Both works have had a strong impact on the development of twentieth-century approaches to music history. If these methodological studies do not always escape a certain dryness, they do raise questions of fundamental importance, and Adler's applications of his own methods show a breadth of interest and awareness, coupled with an individual perceptiveness, that is still noteworthy, as the essay on Mahler attests. With the help of many of the best scholars of his day, he also prepared one of the most highly regarded modern music-histories, the *Handbuch der Musikgeschichte* (first edition 1924), a work distinguished among other qualities for its extensive treatment of modern music. Severe in his estimate of his own creative powers, Adler remained sympathetic to the gifts of others. Many composers – most notably Anton Webern – were his students in music history, and he enjoyed numerous contacts with others, including Bruckner (who was one of his teachers), Brahms, Richard Strauss and Schoenberg, to mention only the more well-known.

Although many tributes were paid to Adler by students, colleagues and friends on such occasions as his sixtieth, seventieth and eightieth birthdays, personal glimpses of the man are rare. Perhaps the finest portrait is found in the memorial article by Carl Engel published in *The Musical Quarterly* shortly after Adler's death in 1941. Engel had known Adler well, and in a few pages creates a lively evocation of their encounters. He draws attention to both the humorous and serious sides of the man in the following passage, and suggests some of those qualities that were essential elements of Adler's friendship with Mahler.

Adler's home in Vienna, Lannerstrasse No. 9, was in the so-called 'cottage' section of the city (the word 'cottage' in Vienna was pronounced as if it were French). A cottage was a detached house of at least two stories, with more or less grounds. The large window of Adler's study looked out on his garden, with shade trees in which birds kept busily singing. His desk was near the window; the grand piano, covered with books and music, stood in a corner; an *étagère* with ferns and flower-pots carried the garden into the room; last but not least there was the sofa for his siesta to which he clung as rigorously as to his afternoon *Jause* – coffee and cake – indispensable to every true Viennese.

In late years, when for two successive seasons I passed several weeks with Adler in Hofgastein, the *Jause* assumed the character of a daily ritual. Any meal with him, even the simplest, required long deliberation in the ordering and not a little persuasiveness in the partaking of it. He believed in having beer precede the wine, an Austrian custom. But he had the waiter bring him a 'beer-warmer' (an iron rod removed from a pot of boiling water and stuck into the beer glass). At first this salutary but barbaric practice horrified me. I never imitated it. Adler was an eminently frugal person. He shunned excesses of all kinds, and deplored them in others. But he had what is called a 'healthy appetite.' He might make a concession and eat a fattened goose liver 'Polish style' – deigning to commend the cuisine – but his favorite dishes were 'national,' from boiled beef with horse-radish and *Kaiserschmarren* to pigs-knuckles, and back again.

Whether it was the main dining rooms of the 'Grand Hotel' and the 'Bristol' in Vienna, or the little café Bachmeyer in Hofgastein, Adler's entrance was the signal for head-waiters to bow to the Herr Hofrat with ceremonial deference, or for the prettiest *Kellnerin* to bestow on the old gentleman her most winning smile. He accepted such homage with charming bonhomie, and not infrequently with a *bon mot*. He loved to elicit laughter when in company.

His serious moods, the unburdening of his mind, the opening of his heart, were formidable things left for moments of strictest intimacy, or for walks through the Gastein valley. Then one became aware of his deep religiousness, of his veneration of nature, of great art, great literature, great music. To the giants of the past he looked up as to heroes even if he found their shining armor bent and bruised in places; with any current *zero*-worship he had little patience. But he took the liveliest interest in such musical innovators as Arnold Schoenberg and Alban Berg. He had Schoenberg participate in the editing of one of the Austrian 'Denkmäler' volumes. Some of the students in his musicological seminar later distinguished themselves as 'advanced' composers.

One could but envy Adler's liberality, his rectitude, his uncompromising honesty, his unaffected modesty. His knowledge of human foibles was uncanny. It made him not only the most sympathetic and tolerant of friends and mentors, but also the kindest, the most touchingly affectionate. He held a lofty conception of family ties and family obligations. However hesitatingly he might embark on some delicate subject, he was sure to end up in perfect and, if necessary, brutal frankness. But the last impression one carried away from any argument with him, was his desire to help, to clarify an idea, to further a cause. He was unselfishness personified.[4]

Adler's study of Mahler was undertaken at the request of Anton Bettelheim, the editor of an annual series that presented extended articles on recently deceased figures. The essay was completed in October 1913 and published the following year. Revised slightly in 1915, it was reissued in book form by Universal Edition in 1916. A so-called 'second edition', which was in fact an unaltered reprint, appeared in 1921.

As Adler anticipated, some of the factual details of his work have proved to be its least durable component. In the present translation I have tried, by drawing upon Adler's original notes, to identify his sources as fully as possible. In the case of outright errors, resulting from slips on the part of the author, lack of information or faulty sources, I have corrected the text and indicated the changes made in my notes. In disputed matters, and in situations in which additional material affects Adler's conclusions, I have sought to provide the pertinent facts in the accompanying annotations. In general, even in cases where Adler's views may now seem most debatable, I have limited myself to indicating differing interpretations. A translation should not, in my view, serve as a platform for the opinions of the translator. Like the early biographers of Mozart and Haydn, I believe Adler merits as straightforward a presentation as possible. One may sometimes disagree but one should always listen.

No music could be included in the original work but, in order to make some of the specific points of Adler's discussion of Mahler's works more immediately comprehensible, a number of examples have been added. These are naturally limited to rather brief passages but I do not believe that the reader will find any difficulties in locating the more extended sections of works cited in the available scores. The chronological table has been completely revised, without editorial comment, in the light of the most recent research. It retains, however, its original highly condensed character and where possible follows Adler's original outline and text. A summary bibliography and an index have been supplied by the translator.

My own study originally appeared in an abbreviated form in the July 1972 issue of *The Musical Quarterly,* and subsequently in its complete form in a German translation by Dr Herta Singer-Blaukopf, published in 1978 as the first volume in the Bibliothek der Internationalen Gustav Mahler Gesellschaft. It is presented now for the first time as it was originally conceived, that is, as a companion and complement to Adler's own work. All deletions in the earlier English version have been restored and some corrections and additions have been incorporated into the present text.

GUSTAV MAHLER

by Guido Adler

FOREWORD
[to the edition of 1916]

This study of Gustav Mahler, published in 1914 in volume XVI of
the *Biographisches Jahrbuch und deutscher Nekrolog,* appears
here in unaltered form.[1] As the editor of the *Jahrbuch,* Dr Anton
Bettelheim, pointed out in his foreword, the manuscript had already been turned over to the printers at the beginning of October
1913. I see no reason to introduce modifications in my work here.
Abbreviations or interpolations would change its proportions and
alter its over-all plan. The essay was the result of long preliminary
studies and of experiences and observations connected with my
friend from his youth to his grave. Hindered only by living in different places, our friendship remained firmly constant. A writer's
assertion that 'no one truly or fully knew Gustav Mahler'[2] I
consider only a voluntary confession of that author. One who
could follow the artist and man in decades-long, familiar inter-
course, who was accustomed to the most intimate exchange of
ideas and belonged to the same cultural circle, perhaps may be
more justly allowed to advance the claim of having gained insight
into Mahler's inmost being. But an outcome such as this cannot be
as fully achieved through personal relations as it can be refined
and confirmed through an approach that is both systematic and
aesthetic.

The lack of such treatment in the literature of musical biography is altogether monstrous and a cancer on our scholarship. Only
someone who can trace the scarlet thread through the life and
works of an artist like Mahler can fathom his complex spiritual
paths and reveal his human and artistic nature. At the same time
one need not stress that a friend's love is not obstructive and does
not blind one. Scholarly conscience and fidelity to truth are
further protections against dissimulation and vain misrepresenta-
tion of the facts of the case. The surest preventatives are historical
schooling and scholarly experience. An amplification of this study
would have required the creation of an entirely new, completely
fresh work. That this was not necessary I will assert publicly.
Expansion or padding does not enhance the value of a work. Any

15

discussion of my personal relations was excluded on the ground that my intention was to view the subject from a higher plane. At the present moment the material is not yet suitable for a strictly historical work. In my observations and statements, perhaps the future will require no alterations. In the chronological table I was able to incorporate some not-unimportant corrections based on documentary evidence and reliable reports. Otherwise this commemorative essay remains unchanged. May it help to further and enhance the understanding of Gustav Mahler's presence and work in wider circles.

Guido Adler

Vienna, September 1915

GUSTAV MAHLER

In the biographies of composers, in the depiction of their struggles and strivings and of the controversies about the evaluation of their work and their individuality, the history of music contains an unmistakable element of military history. In the musical arena, party passions are heightened by the ways of expressing the feelings and moods communicated by musical works and by the different modes of understanding the performance of compositions that show various tendencies and styles. With the continuing growth of individualism from the Renaissance up to our own day, with the spread of subjectivism in the music of the nineteenth century, the feuds have become increasingly pointed, the antagonism between partisans and adversaries increasingly sharp. Since the seventeenth century, especially heated battles have been waged in the sphere of opera; the battle-axe, wielded now in behalf of a composition or composer, now in behalf of a singer of either sex, has never rested. Thus it is not surprising that Gustav Mahler's sharply-defined artistic personality met with opposition of all kinds in its exalted struggle to achieve the loftiest and purest musical ideals and in its determined intervention in behalf of the greatest possible perfection in the reproduction of the art-works of our own and past times. What was and is strange is the kind of attack to which both the creative and re-creative artist was exposed, for which a partial explanation, but no justification, is found in the baser instincts, the malice, of enemies as they appear in nearly all spheres of public life, and in none more than music, where the 'sensitivity' of our period has taken an almost pathological turn. The degree of heat and animosity of the venomous may also be explained in part by the inexorably aggressive will of Mahler, which spared neither himself nor others when there was a question of realizing his deepest and highest artistic convictions. Removed now from party partiality and hatred, today the human and artistic portrait of Mahler can be sketched and the attempt made to place his work in the gallery of history. Although the task is difficult, and we still stand close to the environment that

17

surrounded and included him, it may still be possible, through loving penetration, to grasp the nature of the artist, and, with the aid of historical parallels, to characterize the position that he occupied. Oracular value judgments will not be offered: they change with time and taste. The artist and the man will be revealed as an individual and in his reciprocal relationships, and, in addition, his work will be characterized as clearly as is possible within a brief outline, for more cannot be presented here.

Those who peruse the appended 'chronological table' attentively (see pp. 118-19ff – it is advisable to read it in advance) will be familiar with the external outline of his life and work. Dates speak. The expression *saxa loquuntur* may be applied here to the fixed, plain, dry dates and events as they appear in this absolutely clear-cut form. For me, who in friendly sympathy attended the life and work of Mahler, the compilation of these dates from documents, reports and the literature, was like viewing a silhouette of his whole presence. Unfortunately the physical form of this presence had to disappear before its rich soul had fully communicated and expressed itself, and before its spirit had completed that which it still had to say to the world. His whole life was dismembered by the sudden breaking off of that which had been begun and which was always freshly begun again, and only his almost gigantic energy permitted him to wrest a nine-pointed symphonic crown from *Moira* [fate] together with a series of smaller works.

From his youthful years he had to count on earning his own bread, even though his parents were most intent upon helping him and providing him support. In spite of their limited means, they strove to grant their children a careful rearing and a solid education. The boy grew up in the nationally isolated German-speaking enclave of Iglau;[3] he found rich musical nourishment in the folk songs of both the races among whom he spent his youth. His imagination was excited by woodland scenes cloaked in legends and by the happy activity of the garrison, the bugle-calls of which acquired symbolic meaning for him. Morning and evening calls, assembly and drill motives were in him transformed into sound-images that were solidified around the figure of the old German common foot-soldier. They emerge again and again in vivid re-creations in both the songs and instrumental works of later times, as in 'Revelge', 'Der Tamboursg'sell', 'Der schildwache Nachtlied', 'Lied der Verfolgten im Turm', 'Wo die schönen

Trompeten blasen', in the first and third movements of the Third Symphony, in the variation movement of the Fourth etc. This background also explains Mahler's partiality for march rhythms of all types; they are found again and again in his work, accompanying joy and sorrow, with the most beautiful transfiguration found in the first movement of the Fifth Symphony, the passionately agitated funeral march in C-sharp minor, which is almost an intensification of the mood in the movement of the same type in the 'Eroica' of Beethoven.

The impressions of Mahler's youth extend like a scarlet thread through the creations of his entire life. He held fast to them with moving constancy, just as he remained loyal and grateful to everyone who had ever shown him kindness or of whom he supposed this to be so. In piety he remained constant to his family and, after the death of his parents, almost paternally looked after the education of his brothers and sisters. He himself was filled with an indefatigable passion for education. He acquired books of all sorts, with a special predilection for poetry and philosophy. For some time he even thought of devoting himself also to poetry.[4] The musical instruction in his homeland did not extend beyond the basic elements. Endowment was more evident than accomplishment when, at the age of fifteen, he came to the Conservatory in Vienna. Here, although he had good teachers in piano playing and harmony, his introduction to the higher theoretical subjects (counterpoint and composition) was anything but profound and purposeful. His talent had to overcome this defective education, and only years later, through inflexible application and determined independent study, could Mahler remedy these deficiencies.[5] The comprehension of the youth was so quick that his course of instruction was dispatched in leaps and bounds. He drew the greatest profit from the stimulating activity of the Director of the institution,[6] for the latter created an especially effective model through the performance of chamber music. The 'Hellmesberger Quartet' was a greater influence on us than all instruction. The performance of quartets from Beethoven's last period created deeper impressions than anything then offered in Vienna, and also stylistically affected all students of composition.[7] Added to this were the orchestra rehearsals of the Conservatory under the leadership of the Director. The atmosphere of the *Musikverein*,[8] with its limited means and its admirable sense of dedication, was beneficial in relation to the reproduction of musical works, and the best conductors came out of the Vienna school at that time. Mahler could not hear much, for his means were more than limited. Almost all of the operas that in the course of time he later had to direct, to 'bring out' as best he could, he first became acquainted with through individual study. Thus he could remain original in his conception and stylistically feel his way into, and become familiar with, each work on the strength of his own intuition. In the endlessly varied shadings of the Vienna Philharmonic he could become acquainted with the most magnificent orchestral sound (even the fleeting, rare glimpse suffices for the genius and opens up to him a perspective beyond the reach of the eye). When, in the narrowest artistic alleys of little Austrian provincial towns, he had to bring operas to the footlights with a third of the required instrumental forces and, with a total lack of the less common orchestral instruments, had to rewrite, transpose and adjust parts,[9] his inner ear longed for complete realization and equitable artistic performance as one who is thirsty longs for water. There he became acquainted with a misery as oppressive as that of a father who cannot feed his children. These privations, when Mahler was placed at the head of full-strength, well-situated and funded institutions, had the corresponding effect of causing him to require the greatest degree of devotion to service from the forces placed at his disposal; for, in the service of art or a work, no demand seemed too great to him in order to achieve the achievable, not for the sake of outer success but for the satisfaction of the inner impulse and for the fulfillment of the duty that was sacred to him.

At the age of twenty-three[10] he entered artistic institutions that could satisfy higher demands, as second conductor in Kassel, then in Prague and Leipzig. There he directed operas by Weber, Marschner, Meyerbeer (Kassel), by Cherubini, Mozart, Beethoven, Wagner, Gluck (Prague) and even Mozart and Wagner cycles (Leipzig). He prepared fresh productions of the most difficult works and as a concert conductor even undertook the Ninth Symphony of Beethoven. He created such a deep impression with this performance in Prague (at that time Professor at the German University, I was in attendance) that at the instigation of the pathologist Philipp Knoll, a political leader of the Germans in Bohemia, an address was presented to him by the academic com-

munity, with the participation of other circles of society; it gave
memorable expression to the admiration for and gratitude to the
twenty-five-year-old conductor. At a music festival arranged in
Kassel the preceding summer Mahler had also received enthusiastic approval. The ambitious young artist sought a larger, more
independent, sphere of activity and found it as Director of the
Royal Opera in Budapest. Having worked in second positions in
Prague (with *Kapellmeister* Slansky[11] in the first) and in Leipzig
(with Arthur Nikisch), he felt that he had a strong enough
impetus to raise himself to a first position. His goal was to be able
to direct works that corresponded to his inclinations, and which
he could choose freely. The theaters in Leipzig and Prague are
private theaters, and although they are subsidized (by the munici-
pality in Leipzig, by the *Landesausschuss*[12] as the 'Königliches
deutsches Landestheater' in Prague), the lessees are more or less
free to make their own arrangements, especially in engaging personnel, and have complete freedom in their artistic direction.
Angelo Neumann in Prague and Max Staegemann in Leipzig
were skillful theater managers and knew how to hold their
ground. To do so in Prague was no easy matter, since in that
nationally divided city the German theater had to contend with
the competition of the Czech National Theater, received a signifi-
cantly smaller subsidy and had a much smaller public, although
the latter was and is very well-disposed to the theater. The
orchestra was not first-class and could not be improved in the
manner that seemed desirable to Mahler and to others. In both
cities Mahler was able to become familiar with the ingenuities of
an 'impresario in angustie'.[13] He did not adapt himself to them
and all his life remained a direct man pursuing purely artistic
goals. He would have preferred to proceed like the great Handel,
who, as opera director, immediately removed unfit singers or even
held an insubordinate singer out of the window as if he planned to
drop her. Serious and zealous actors found in him a most devoted instructor and guide. Thus an inquiry directed to me by the
Prague-born David Popper, then Professor of 'cello in Budapest
(made in the name of several influential artists in Budapest,
Edmund von Mihalovich among them), could be answered with
the reassuring report and confident declaration that as artist and
man Mahler was entirely suitable for the post of opera director,
and that his organizational talent would in any case grow.[14] My

conviction was confirmed in the most brilliant fashion, and could once more be given full expression when Mahler was later to come to Vienna and the *Intendant* Baron Bezecny turned to me with regard to his doubts.

In Pest there was arduous work ahead: opened in 1884, the Royal Hungarian Opera – previously opera and drama were combined in the 'National Theater' – had at the end of 1887 'reached its first artistic and financial crisis'.[15] Mahler put a quick end to the guest and star system and with the forces at his disposal sought to create an ensemble that would offer unified productions; in conformity with regulation, these were in Hungarian. In the two years of his activity he succeeded to the point where he 'guided the unschooled material to an astonishing stylistic sureness' (Report of Dr Béla Diósy). Only in highly dramatic works was he forced to draw temporarily upon German singers, and they had to sing in the Italian language. Such were the heights to which the waves of chauvinism had risen. The repertoire embraced operas – German, French, Italian and also Hungarian – which only a first-class institution is in a position to perform in a worthy manner. 'The high artistic level of these performances – in which Mahler's remarkable talent for stage management was also evident – was never again reached by the Royal Opera.' 'The performances of the orchestra were brought to a perfection previously unsuspected.' The theater was 'restored to health financially, and lifted artistically into its most brilliant era'.[16] The best musicians of the city – von Mihalovich, Hubay, Koessler, von Herzfeld and others – offered enthusiastic support, as did the public, in so far as they were not adherents of the *ancien régime*, did not belong to discarded native forces, or oppose the 'German' artist for chauvinistic reasons. But the inflexible energy devoted purely to artistic goals, and the harsh discipline that did not spare personal ambitions, also resulted in ill will. When Mahler's superior, the government commissioner Franz von Beniczky, who had followed his Director's devoted activity with appreciation, exchanged his post with that of a High Count of the Pest *Comitates*, the one-armed piano virtuoso and composer Count Géza Zichy, 'a haughty magnate', was appointed *Intendant*. The latter 'wished to take over wholly or in part the business of management himself',[17] and Mahler, after some resistance, was forced to yield. Later Count Zichy candidly admitted

that forcing Mahler out was the greatest mistake of his administration. Too late! But from the Magyar city Mahler took with
him an especially precious success: the recognition of Brahms,
who had been unwillingly taken to a performance of *Don Giovanni* conducted by Mahler. In front of the theater Brahms said: 'No
one does *Don Giovanni* the way I like it. If I wish to enjoy it, I lie
down on the sofa and read the score.' During the performance:
'Excellent! Splendid! Magnificent! Yes, that's it, finally. What a
devil of a fellow!'[18] Immediately after the first act Koessler and von
Herzfeld had to guide him to the stage, where he embraced the
young conductor and, beaming, declared this to be the best performance of *Don Giovanni* that he had heard. How often during
Mahler's subsequent activity in Hamburg and Vienna were artists
and friends of art, with an appreciation similar to, or the same as,
that of Brahms, able to experience such efficacy! But the avowal
of such enthusiasm is to be expected only from those who are
unprejudiced and devoid of hate or envy!

On the day that Mahler tendered his resignation in Pest, he was
called to Hamburg by a telegram from Pollini. For six years
Mahler was active there as first conductor, and with able forces
could present model performances that made him appear in the
eyes of Hans von Bülow as the revitalizer of the Hamburg Opera.
A laurel wreath of the critical music-master, who was feared all
over Germany, bore the inscription: 'To the Pygmalion of the
Hamburg Opera – from Hans von Bülow'. When Bülow felt
himself ailing and sick and retired from the leadership of the sub-
scription concerts of the 'Hamburg Friends of Music' (1893), he
indicated Mahler as a suitable successor and the latter served as
conductor in 1894/5. As early as 1885 Bülow had also cited
Mahler – then only twenty-five years old! – among the other candi-
dates, Weingartner, Nicodé and Zumpe, who appeared suitable
to him in connection with the question of filling the post of
Kapellmeister at the Berlin Opera (*Briefe*, vol. 6, p. 359).[19]
Nevertheless, some dissenting voices were also raised in Hamburg,
as is understandable with an artist as highly energetic and far-
reaching as Mahler. Deeper causes of dissent have not yet been
discovered and it would be difficult indeed to gain an accurate
picture from comments pro and con in the newspapers. A well-
qualified party has declared that 'under Mahler Hamburg was a
center of progressive musical life'.[20] The artists who wished to

work seriously were attached to him with respect, and thus some whom he called – Anna von Mildenburg, Bertha Foerster-Lauterer, Leopold Demuth, Erik Schmedes – followed him to the center of his new activity. In Vienna they found a place where, under the leadership of the 'Artistic Director of the Imperial and Royal Court Opera', they succeeded to new achievements and triumphs. For several months Mahler was active as conductor and deputy of the director Jahn; thereafter he was entrusted with independent leadership. Among male soloists with considerable powers he found Winkelmann, Reichenberg, Schrödter, Van Dyck, Ritter, Reichmann, Hesch. Among female soloists: Renard, Walker, Sedlmair. The other conductors were Hans Richter, Johann Nepomuk Fuchs, Josef Hellmesberger, Jr and Josef Bayer. The last three departed in the course of the year. Richter retired from his post on 2 March 1900 and found in England a sphere of activity in the exercise of which he did not have to be subordinated to a younger colleague. The reasons for the departure of the Court Opera conductor lay in conditions in which he, who had been active in Vienna for twenty-five years, could no longer see his way clearly. The party supporting him would not permit themselves a fair and just evaluation of the accomplishments of Mahler and found a natural reinforcement in the political party that came to power in the Vienna town hall,[21] in so far as it concerned itself at all with artistic matters. For the latter the artistic motive was not decisive but rather the personal, the blind fanaticism that, since Mahler had gone over to Catholicism before he assumed his office in Vienna, could not be turned against his lineage. Adherents of this party in the press, and also some opponents in the liberal or pseudo-liberal press, who, through attacks of this sort, wished to show themselves independent and 'party-less', joined a solid opposition, which now launched its poisonous darts from this side or that.[22] Mahler worked on vigorously and firmly as before. In addition to the forces from Hamburg mentioned above he obtained the female artists Hilgermann, Gutheil-Schoder, Kittel, Weidt, Forst, Bland, Cahier, Kurz; the male artists Slezak, Weidemann, Mayr and others; appointed the conductors Franz Schalk, Bruno Walter, Francesco Spetrino and Julius Lehnert, who were retained, while Ferdinand Löwe, Gustav Brecher and Alexander von Zemlinsky departed after short periods of activity. Among the previous conductors,

Fuchs, through his death in 1899, and Josef Hellmesberger, Jr departed. Among well-known singers Dippel, Renard, Van Dyck, Reichenberg, Naval, Winkelmann, Ritter, Forster, Sedlmair and others left in the course of time.[23] Whoever is familiar with the personalities of the opera from this period will recognize that the guiding principle for appointment and release was regard for the possibility of orderly placement in a unified organic ensemble. The departures are to be explained partly as a result of the in- adequacy of individual powers that must be expected and demanded in relation to particular productions, partly as a result of the powerful competition that American stages give to the court theaters of the Old World when, with their fees, they catch popular singers in their gilded cages. Never, however, was a personal motive decisive. Mahler most deeply deplored the depar- ture, by retirement, of Winkelmann, a singer of great style who was serious and eager to serve. In certain years of Mahler's direc- torial administration an increased number of guest performers was necessary (thus especially in the 1902/3 season), since, because of various repertoire difficulties, he could not often absent himself in order to find a suitable selection. Then when he did travel abroad, especially to Germany, for the sake of perform- ances of his works (none of his symphonies was allotted a first performance in Vienna during his lifetime, since he was too high- minded to use his position for personal ends), he had the op- portunity at various places to fill gaps in his personnel. He went out of his way to make the ensemble as complete as possible, to be in a position to provide each new première or new production with a double cast and to avoid disagreeable alterations in the fixed re- pertoire. With painful care Mahler took the lead in supplement- ing the instrumentalists of the Court Opera Orchestra and making new appointments, and in providing for raises in their in- come. His special 'social' care was expended on them as well as on the chorus and the supers.[24]

At the time he assumed the directorship, the orchestra was, in spite of its pre-eminence, in need of restoration. Step by step the ground had to be won, fortified and extended. Discipline had be- come lax in the last years of the directorship of Wilhelm Jahn, since this experienced opera conductor had been ill, and the other conductors, in spite of their artistic qualities, possessed neither the powers nor sufficient authority to make changes. *Laissez aller, laissez faire* had crept in and the consequences were disagreeably apparent even in the Wagner performances led by Hans Richter. Thus Mahler initiated new productions and directed the Wagner operas without cuts. *Die Meistersinger, Tristan und Isolde, The Ring*, then the earlier *Rienzi, Der fliegende Holländer, Tannhäuser* and *Lohengrin* appeared one after the other, complete transformations of the earlier productions, in new, artistic raiment. For these productions he associated himself with Alfred Roller,[25] whom he had met in the circle of artists who frequented the house of the painter Karl Moll, the stepfather of his fiancée and subsequent wife; with the artists of this circle, Gustav Klimt and Kolo Moser among them, Mahler had friendly personal and artistic relations. Thus there came into being a harmony of convictions and aspirations, which was decisive for the Court Opera in the field of scenery and which also set a standard outside of Austria. Mahler, the conductor, dramatist, stage manager and vocal coach, who determined and directed the entire performance down to the smallest detail, had found in Roller a colleague who realized the scenic representation in a manner that was in complete accord with his artistic views as General Director. The visual artist sometimes subordinated himself, sometimes drew the Director aside and was able to change his mind.[26] Although in musical-dramatic matters there was no experimentation (in spite of frequent changes during rehearsal), experiments were attempted in scenic-visual realization, which were valuable in themselves and also pointed the way to higher achievement. The summit that both Mahler and Roller longed to reach was unfortunately not granted them; after Mahler had departed, Roller soon took his leave. In such service only artistic natures of the same type are able to create a unity: the operatic trade can only be ennobled into a true artistic occupation through an ideal concord between all parties. In the complete harmoniousness of the visual and tone colors of the scenes, in the necessary co-ordination of spatial limitation and expansion with dramatic requirements and with the poetry of word and melody, the décor of *Tristan* was truly overpowering in its effect, without in any way impairing its function through obtrusiveness. The experiments also extended to the newly produced Mozart operas, in which the problems were not entirely solved. But musically these performances belonged stylistically to the purest ever presented in the Vienna Opera, or

possibly on any of the stages of the world – judging from knowledge gained from direct observation and from the descriptions of
contemporaries. Even from past descriptions the historian cannot
attest to a higher consummation of stylistically tasteful reproduction in the various schools. *Così fan tutte, Die Zauberflöte, Die
Entführung aus dem Serail, Le Nozze di Figaro, Don Giovanni* –
each in succession was rejuvenated, and above all it was these
performances in Vienna which brought about the Mozart renaissance, which in our time proved to be both reservoir and fountain
of youth for the ebbing tide of opera production. The introduction of the judgment scene from Beaumarchais' drama in the
Figaro of Da Ponte clarified the action in terms of the Beaumarchais fiction. As I have sought to demonstrate elsewhere (*Zeitschrift der Internationalen Musikgesellschaft,* 5),[27] the dramatic
rearrangement of Weber's *Euryanthe* seems an improvement to
me. Works of Gluck, Rossini, Meyerbeer, Halévy, Verdi and
Goldmark were also newly produced, as well as comic operas such
as *Zar und Zimmermann, Fra Diavolo, La Dame blanche, Die
lustigen Weiber von Windsor;* then *Der Freischütz, Falstaff,
Iphigénie en Aulide* and *Fidelio.* The last was given an incomparable rendering, with the transfer of the first scene into a
chamber in Rocco's dwelling, the insertion of the third *Leonora*
overture between the dungeon and closing scenes, after the duet
of the married couple, and the *Fidelio* overture played at the
beginning of the work.

With the last performance of this work of Beethoven, fitted out
with Roller's décor (especially characteristic in the *petit bourgeois*
room, the gloomy dungeon court and the free landscape), with
the finest details of the musical performance cared for (as everywhere in Mahler productions), impressive in its grandeur, deeply
affecting in the depth and power of its re-creation, Mahler bade
farewell to the home of his endeavors. On 15 October 1907 he
directed for the last time in the house in which on the first
occasion, on 21 July 1897, he had conducted *Lohengrin.* The
public was not aware that Mahler would not direct in the opera
house again. He wished to avoid any demonstration. Between the
first *Lohengrin* and the last *Fidelio* lay an extended period within
which Mahler's capacities and mastery had not changed, but in
which political agitation and subversion by his opponents had
made the insensitive and vacillating section of the public blind

and deaf to his achievements.[28] This is frequently the case, and at
many places. In many respects the Viennese are like the ancient
Romans: *novarum rerum cupidi.* Both the theatrical and the
higher governmental authorities have to reckon with this characteristic fondness for innovation. The new in itself seems salutary,
even when it breaks away in the most arbitrary manner from the
previously existing, as now happened in the Opera, even with the
superb *Fidelio* production of Mahler, which was demolished and
reconstructed by the new management![29] From the treasure of the
older operatic repertoire Mahler had also restored the *Iphigénie
en Aulide* of Gluck to blooming life. He might have resuscitated
further treasures if his activity had not met with a premature end.

The choice of new works proved difficult during his activity in
Vienna. That he had a true eye for effective new operas he had
already proved in Pest, where he produced Mascagni's *Cavalleria
Rusticana* for the first time outside of Italy. But the output of con-
temporary operas was then even poorer than today. Richard
Strauss' *Feuersnot* and Pfitzner's *Die Rose vom Liebesgarten* were
the best German operas at his disposal. *Salome* remained forbid-
den to him, since at that time the consent of the court officials
could not be obtained. *Lobetanz* by Thuille, *Der Bärenhäuter* by
Siegfried Wagner, *Die Kriegsgefangene* by Goldmark, *Donna
Diana* by Reznicek, *Die Abreise* and *Flauto solo* by D'Albert, and
Das war ich by Leo Blech, were the further (meager) yields from
the works of German artists. The following Slavs had their turns:
Tchaikovsky with *Eugene Onegin, Iolanthe* and *Pique Dame*,
Smetana with *Dalibor*, Rubinstein with *The Demon.* Newly
introduced Italian works included the *Bohème* of Leoncavallo
and also that by Puccini, *Fedora* by Giordano, *Le donne curiose*
by Wolf-Ferrari and *Madama Butterfly* by Puccini. Frenchmen
given premières included Saint-Saëns (*Samson et Dalila*), Bizet
(*Djamileh*), Delibes (*Lakmé*), Charpentier (*Louise*), Erlanger (*Le
Juif polonais*) and Offenbach (*Les Contes d'Hoffmann*). Austri-
ans: Hugo Wolf (*Der Corregidor*), Zemlinsky (*Es war einmal*), J.
Forster (*Der dot mon*), J. Reiter (*Der Bundschuh*). Fourteen new
ballets were given, and from the older operatic domain Haydn's
Der Apotheker, Mozart's *Zaïde* and Lortzing's *Die Opernprobe*
were adopted. In addition the balance of the permanent operatic
repertoire was freshened up, in so far as time and circumstances
permitted. Mahler's plans were far-reaching and he dispensed

with many works in the repertoire reluctantly, or felt painfully the unsatisfactory state of the production of this or that opera taken over from the preceding period. Gluck, Marschner and Weber were to be more fully represented, Berlioz given his say. Many gaps were to be filled and the insatiable theater-Moloch appeased. 'Instead of a completed whole, as I dreamed, I leave behind a fragmentary, incomplete work, as man is fated to do,' Mahler said in an over-modest manner in his farewell message 'to the esteemed members of the Court Opera'.

My efforts could not always be crowned with success. No one is so at the mercy of 'the intractability of the material', 'the treachery of the object' as the practicing artist. But I have always staked my whole being, subordinated myself to the work at hand, my inclinations to duty. I have not spared myself and thus could demand from others the exertion of all their powers. In the press of battle and the heat of the moment neither you nor I were spared wounds and misunderstandings. But if a work succeeded, if a problem was solved, we forgot all the toil and trouble and felt ourselves richly rewarded – even without outer tokens of success. We have all progressed, and with us the institution that was the object of all our endeavors.[30]

Thus, in tranquillity, the artist could speak with regard to intention, ability and accomplishment.

What base attacks were directed against them! Every insubordination of a member of the company was exaggerated into an 'affair', in which only the 'tyranny', 'whim' and 'despotism' of the Director were blamed. 'Serious complaints' were raised – against everything that happened, against repertoire, acceptance of new works, appointment of conductors, artistic improvement of the personnel and decline of the ballets. I cite the *ipsissima verba* without doing such people the honor of naming them. Mahler was denied the ability to judge artistic personalities; he was accused of exclusively pursuing personal goals... The accusations rose to monstrous proportions. When he abolished the claque as unworthy of a serious artistic institution, the clapping palms were sorely missed. When he forbade entrance during the performance in order to avoid disturbances, long-standing holders of reserved seats rebelled. Gradually his iron discipline won the upper hand among the personnel, his energy among the public. But all the 'affairs', all the attacks, were only fractions of the opposition, which on artistic grounds was neither explainable nor justifiable. The case became, as Max Burckhard said, a 'Politicum' [an affair

of state].[31] Mahler's pleasure in the work could not be destroyed,
but a disgust appeared that was further strengthened by private
influences.[32] Mahler's creative work, however, was not to be
weakened by having to settle down once more in unfamiliar circumstances. He was rooted in Vienna and Austria. As a universal
artist he still had not lost the narrower feeling for his native country and even if he had to quit the seat of his glorious activity,
retirement alone, which would have provided him with the opportunity to devote more time to the performances of his works,
would have sufficed. Indeed, during the last period of his directorial activity, in addition to his summer holiday, which was
devoted principally to composition, he had absented himself for a
few days several times during the year to obey a summons to direct
one of his works here or there, so that he could give it a hearing.
This also was made a reproach to him and might have been a
valid reproach if in so doing he had neglected his duty. But in
Franz Schalk and Bruno Walter he had suitable deputies for individual performances, and the latter in particular immersed
himself so deeply in Mahler's artistry, conducted himself with such
love and devotion, that Mahler could easily vindicate his sporadic
absence from his official post.

For the benefit of the Philharmonic in the spring of 1900 he
went to Paris and with this body gave there five concerts, the
deficit for which he had to raise with the help of a Viennese
artistic Maecenas.[33] In Vienna he led the concerts of the Philharmonic in the 1898/9, 1899/1900, and 1900/1 seasons. Let us
not go into the question of whether the members were grateful.[34]
Here also he demanded more rehearsals than were customary,
either previously or subsequently. The worst reproach made
against him was the over-intense subjectivity in his execution.
Indeed he 'took' many things differently from others. The
individuality of a Mahler requires the realization of its originality,
which does not always coincide with the usual conception. I myself
have imagined many things – this or that movement, this or that
passage – differently from the way I ultimately heard them. From
such a powerful personality, who in his conception wishes only to
do justice to the work, I will accept a divergence without further
ado. I submit all the more willingly since I have discovered that
different conceptions of a work can be presented by one and the
same interpreter – as I experienced with exaltation from Rubin-

stein and Liszt.[35] We know that Beethoven rendered his own works
in various lights in accordance with his emotional temper and
state of mind. Mahler's arrangement of Beethoven's Ninth Symphony was made into an 'affair'. Following Richard Wagner's
precedent, Mahler had, in order to achieve that clarity which was
to him the highest principle of reproduction, doubled the woodwinds in individual passages, employed a third and fourth pair of
horns and in the last movement employed a third and fourth
trumpet. Now and then, in addition to the natural tones of the
brass instruments in use in Beethoven's time, from the full scale of
the valved instruments Mahler filled in the passages that, in his
view, Beethoven could produce only with gaps on the natural
instruments. This was a bold procedure, which Mahler also
wished to justify (in an open letter to the concert-goers) on the
basis of Beethoven's deafness and the inadequacy of the realization of his intentions. The multiplication of the string instruments
since Beethoven's time requires, as Mahler pointed out, an increase in the winds. He wished 'without arbitrariness and will-
fulness, but also without being misled by any tradition, to enter
into even the apparently insignificant details of Beethoven's intentions, and in performance not allow even the smallest thing
desired by the Master to be sacrificed or submerged in a confused
tumult of sound'. 'Naturally there can be no question of a re-
instrumentation, a modification or even an "improvement" of the
work of Beethoven.'[36] The intention is commendable, but the
means are to be sanctioned only in so far as they match the intention of the reproducer without permitting any pretension to
universal validity to arise – for the alterations of Mahler no more
than for those of Wagner still employed by many conductors of
our time. Since the original of Beethoven continues to be invio-
lably preserved, no lasting detriment can result from this.
Whether interpretation can and should go so far is a question in
itself. The imperfections in the fulfillment of that ideal which
hovers before the composer, and which he wishes to realize in the
work of art, are lasting attendant manifestations of the qualities of
the work. Whether on the whole the latter gains true completion
through such alterations cannot be verified. For the general
public, which usually hardly notices such additions, this question
is of less moment. The matter is one of conscience, which one can
deny neither Wagner nor Mahler. The historian will have to stand

up for the unalloyed preservation of the authentic text; yet he can still recognize the good intention of the clarification without granting it any universal validity.

That Mahler could enter completely into the reproduction of the works of the most diverse masters and times, and that he also brilliantly proved himself in the co-creative completion of musical fragments, is shown in the most startling manner by his work on *Die drei Pintos* of Weber. Weber had occupied himself with his first drafts in the years 1816-21, and still thought of completing the composition in the year of his death (1826). Individual pieces, sketches and fragments are preserved for only the first two acts; Mahler had to step in completely for the third. He did this partly by utilizing compositions of Weber, partly by realizing ideas of Weber and partly by entirely new inventions in Weber's idiom. So fully had the arranger entered into the spirit of the 'tone-weaver' that the Mahler pieces were considered Weberesque and the Weber numbers Mahleresque. Weber's grandson had taken up the plan for the completion again after Meyerbeer had been asked to undertake it some time previously, and had kept the sketches for years without proceeding to carry out the wishes of the family. Charming in individual parts, the whole falls short of Weber as we know him from *Der Freischütz, Euryanthe* and *Oberon.*[37] For theaters in which comic operas of the smaller, lighter genre have a suitable niche, the newly obtained opera would still be effective. It is not very significant in the total picture of Weber's artistry. It is a trial by fire for Mahler's stylistic powers of identification, for he was then on the point of enlarging his own style in the sketches for his Second Symphony. The work on *Die drei Pintos* was finished in the briefest possible time[38] and from the first performance in Leipzig (20 January 1888) met with approval and success in many German cities. It was also performed in Vienna in January 1889. Mahler modestly deferred to Weber's grandson, who had taken an active hand in the libretto. When Mahler was Director in Vienna, he did not perform this opera. He did not want to have it appear that the production was due to his own participation in the work. As devoted as he was in friendship, here also he avoided exercising protection for the sake of 'friendship' (*Freunderlschaft,* a Viennese expression),[39] or allowing himself to be influenced by personal considerations, although he did discuss matters with his friends. From his earlier days in Vienna he still encountered Dr Emil

Freund, the ever-faithful lawyer, who now performed the pleasant duty of taking over the 'initial administration of the estate',[40] the archaeologist Dr Fritz Löhr and the poet Dr Siegfried Lipiner, Librarian of the Parliament. The last, with his profound cultivation and the buoyancy of his imaginative life, exerted a powerful influence on the friend of his youth. Philosophic themes were considered with fervor and deep penetration by these friends, world literature in its most powerful manifestations taken up in detail, and religious questions discussed with solemn severity.

To pursue his reading, no free minute that Mahler saved in his difficult and demanding profession was left unused. To refresh himself he examined masterpieces of music literature and buried himself in the study of Bach's works, which he placed before him to recover and strengthen himself from the confusion of the day. He zealously read the Denkmäler der Tonkunst, on the Board of Directors of which (in Vienna) he was an effective member.[41] Of friends from the first Viennese days Hugo Wolf was still living, but unfortunately no longer open to a close relationship.[42] The brothers Krzyzanowski (Rudolf the musician, Heinrich the writer) had moved to Germany. The highly gifted young musician Hans Rott, the most gifted of all of us who belonged to the Conservatory circle in the seventies, had died early.[43] Mahler won new friends, and in cultured circles the number of devoted admirers multiplied rapidly and was augmented from abroad. The artists have already been mentioned. Among poets and writers the following may be noted: Gerhart Hauptmann, Hugo von Hofmannsthal, Arthur Schnitzler, Max Burckhard, Hermann Bahr, Felix Salten and Stefan Zweig. Among writers on music: Oskar Bie, Hermann Bischoff, Ernst Decsey, Georg Göhler, Eduard Hanslick, Julius Korngold, E. O. Nodnagel, R. Piper, William Ritter, Ludwig Schiedermair, Arthur Seidl, Richard Specht, Paul Stefan, Max Steinitzer and others. Among musicians (in Vienna): Bruno Walter, Alexander von Zemlinsky, Josef V. von Wöss, J.B. Förster, Arnold Schoenberg, Julius Bittner, Arthur Bodansky, Gustav Brecher, Karl Weigl; (abroad): Richard Strauss (in close friendship), Hans Pfitzner, Max Schillings, Oskar Fried, Wilhelm Kienzl, Willem Mengelberg, Julius Buths, Paul Dukas and a wide range of younger people. Among foreigners Hermann Behn (Hamburg), Paul Clemenceau and Marie-Georges Picquart (the

Minister of War in Paris) also ought to be especially singled out.[44]

As incomplete as this list is, especially with regard to the women who belonged to his domestic coterie, it gives an approximate idea of the circle whose members were more or less closely connected with Mahler. As much as he withdrew, his communications were uncommonly far-flung (and in the last years extended even to America) because of connections in almost all the musical cities of Austria, Germany, England, France, Italy and Russia. He went to America for the first time in December 1907 and directed operas by Mozart and Wagner at the Metropolitan Opera in New York during the 1907/8 season; he returned three times in all, twice after the Philharmonic Society had been reorganized in New York to give concerts under Mahler.[45] He held himself ever more aloof from performances of opera. Spring, summer and a part of the fall he spent in his native land and directed concerts of works by himself and others at various places, especially Munich, Amsterdam, Paris, Rome and several German cities. In the New World his fees were considerable; these had no special attraction for him, but for his family he had to provide a broader material foundation than would have been possible through his pension and his previous savings. With the latter he might have found a livelihood sufficient for himself, especially as he was often called to conduct concerts that brought him substantial sums. He could also expect revenue from his works: certain of his symphonies found publishers who paid well. Since the Gesellschaft zur Förderung deutscher Wissenschaft, Kunst und Literatur in Böhmen [Society for the Advancement of German Science, Art and Literature in Bohemia] had granted the German-Bohemian Mahler a subsidy for the publication of his symphonies in the year 1898 – previously an enthusiastic partisan had arranged for the engraving of the Second Symphony – his works were given the opportunity to gain wider dissemination.[46] Yet another possibility had presented itself to change his sphere of activity and strengthen his income in Vienna. The Conservatory of the Gesellschaft der Musikfreunde was financially pressed and, through encroachments from a party devoid of understanding, had experienced changes in organization and staffing that in no way benefited the institution. The Ministry of Culture and Education raised the subsidy from year to year. It was essential for a man to step in who would be equal to the task of bringing about a change and of leading the institution to those heights on which it had once stood when, even though the means were not yet abundant, the ability and artistry of the leaders had won out over that external limitation. At the request of Minister von Hartel[47] a memorandum was worked out in which the renovation of the institution was considered and proposals were submitted (with respect to organization and the appointment of suitable forces).[48] Mahler was to be named General Director. To the proponents Mahler had pledged that he was prepared to assume this position – it conformed all the more to certain of his inclinations since in his youth he had already intended to teach music.[49] As long as he was Director of the Court Opera, he would accept no honorarium; after giving up the direction of the Opera he would receive a suitable (previously agreed-upon) stipend. Discussions were protracted. The reasons need not be discussed in detail here. In accordance with the proposal, Mahler would have had to watch over the institution, which had previously remained under the administration of the Gesellschaft der Musikfreunde, as a government trustee. Mahler would have had to exercise supervision at the highest level and, in accordance with his wish or judgment, would have undertaken at any time to lead this or that performance. Changes in ministers did not help to settle matters. But when Dr Max Graf Wickenburg undertook the reorganization of the music department and was informed of the memorandum, he applied to Mahler. Disgusted by the disgraceful circumstances that resulted in his resignation [from the Opera], upset by influences from another quarter,[50] Mahler answered the manager Conried's tempting call to America, gave up his intention of accepting the honorable proposal for Vienna and turned down his friendly intermediaries. Mahler now chose to abandon Vienna, and Vienna was forsaken by a friendly genius who had reawakened the old musical city to a powerful new life. A writer (Hagemann) called the departure (without the possibility of knowing that Mahler might have been kept for Vienna even without the Opera) a cultural tragedy.[51] The tragic outcome did not fail to develop. For Mahler, especially as his health was weakened, the three-fold[52] repetition of the voyage to America was fatal. Today Vienna must still bear the heavy consequences of his departure. Mahler would only have had to work through example, and the younger generation would have modeled itself accordingly. His example would have had lasting effects not only in the sphere of reproduction. In his creative art Mahler also belongs to the leading spirits of his time.

To understand truly Mahler's productive and reproductive manner, one must – as with every artist – picture his character to oneself. Creation and re-creation are reflections of the spiritual life; even more, the works are its offspring, its issue, and in the re-creation of musical works, in so far as it is not mechanical, a part of the individual life of the reproducer manifests itself. Mahler's spiritual life was founded on goodness and energy. In the divine mania of the artist as well as in the inexorable impulse to truth in all vital utterances, the firmness of his will reached the point of fanaticism. Like a child he let himself be carried away by the moment, and in such moments his temperament seemed lacking in restraint. Nevertheless his clear intellect was also master of the final consequences of his actions. His will proved itself inflexible, yet he was tender-hearted. His nature was generous and his feeling for fellow creatures, for large and small, for grown-ups and children, childlike; it was touching in friendship, in attachment open, frank to the point of self-abnegation. He could take delight in all things but lose his temper over the slightest matter if it did not conform to his mood of the moment. Sensitive and irritable, he could bear the most violent sorrows without complaint and a moment later become angry over the slightest inconvenience. Over-trusting and communicative with those whom he regarded and acquired as friends, mistrustful and reserved with disagreeable people in whom he found no understanding, he immediately threw the harshest 'truths' into the latters' faces, here and there offending them. This characteristic also accounts for antagonisms, which not infrequently resulted from injured vanity. Mahler wanted to grasp life in all its heights and depths. Tragedy and joy in all their manifestations found an echo in his heart. This fact explains why, in his symphonies, the sublime is followed directly by the greatest plainness, the commonplace. To him music seemed also to ennoble the latter; or he wanted, through the reflection of fortuitous happenings, to grasp all phases of life in sound and reproduce them in a temporal order within the musical work. In this respect he let himself be led by feeling and answered for himself as a clear, reasonable person. 'The intellect errs, feeling does not' was his artistic credo.[53] In art, in artistic matters, he let himself be guided by inner instinct, by impulse: it must be so. Thus although he managed 'to make no concessions artistically', humanly he did. The man in him was soft as butter, the artist inflexible in the pursuit of the ideal that hovered before him.

Mahler was neither complete pessimist nor total optimist. He thought the best of everyone as long as he was not convinced of the contrary. His experience with most journalism and with one concert-society[54] or another made him skeptical, but not self-conscious or prejudiced. To be sure, he read Schopenhauer and Nietzsche with partiality (he subsequently turned away from the latter) and buried himself in Dostoevsky's works. From youth he was familiar with the classics of world literature; in later years Goethe was closest to him; in his youth he was especially fond of E.T.A. Hoffmann (whose *Kapellmeister* 'Kreisler' left many traces in Mahler or, more accurately, provided many analogies, such as his over-excited disposition and his lack of composure) and also Hölderlin and Jean Paul, whose *Titan* gave the First Symphony its poetic accompaniment and at first even its title.[55] In his symphonies one finds the negation of life as the decisive characteristic now and then, most markedly in the Sixth, called the 'Tragic', but even here brightness, as in the trio of the second movement, or wild gaiety are found, as well as reverie and glimpses into beloved regions (third movement). It is a mistake to believe that Mahler 'hated the little amusements of humanity'.[56] On the contrary, he was childishly delighted with them; at the time of his most arduous directorial problems he hopped and footed it in the house of friends and struck up merry tunes in his smallest circle. Full affirmation of life speaks from many movements of his symphonies: thus, among others, in the third and fourth movements of the Fifth Symphony, and in the Fourth Symphony, in which he celebrates heavenly joys similar to those for which the spirit of the people longs. The sensual joy of the Viennese penetrates here and there, united with the joy in the sound of music of his native place, and harmonizes with the dark vehemence that dominates whole sections and movements. A man who works with such joy, who celebrates unwavering strength with as much force as in the Seventh, has in himself an inextinguishable fund of vital energy and hope. All his life he was a 'God-seeker' and a wrestler after truth. In his compositions also he seeks to struggle through to a comprehension of existence, to the realization of his highest goals.

What knowledge denied him, he sought at least to experience artistically, or (if such an expression is permissible) to intuit from afar. He did not wish to philosophize in the work of art but only to write good music that would give artistic shape to his moods. He was stimulated by philosophic trains of thought without wishing to philosophize in music (which is in itself impossible). Since, following Beethoven's example, he seeks to touch the sublime with his art, he wishes in individual movements of his works to intuit, behold, descry the ultimate ends of primal knowledge – without being able to grasp them, just as science cannot explain them. In the Third Symphony (a 'Summer Morning Dream'), after he first listens to the awakening of nature in the first movement ('Pan awakes'), he tells himself in the following movements of the flowers, the woodland animals, man, the angels, and then in an incomparably magnificent Adagio (final movement) 'What love tells me' or 'What God tells me'! Thus to him God and love are synonymous. A pessimist does not think and feel like this.

Everywhere he sings of love, the divine in man; it even forms the connecting link between the first and second parts of the Eighth, between the hymn 'Veni creator spiritus' and the concluding part of Goethe's *Faust,* the two textual foundations of the symphonic edifice. The highest consequence of contemplation of the world and of artistic reproduction in all of his works is the communication of love in all of its reflections. As sunlight is prismatically refracted, so love is divided, not into seven but into countless, into infinite, hues and shades. Mahler does not avoid reproducing even a kind of love that is sentimental, bordering on the banal, as in the posthorn solo of the third movement of the Third, or the blunt sort of the common foot-soldier and horseman. A monotheistic faith is found in Mahler, which, regardless of whether he may harbor doubts at one moment or in many, is at one with all denominational manifestations of religion and also, as paradoxical as it may seem, with pantheistic views: he even ingenuously depicts superstitions without finding fault with them, making a travesty of them or treating them ironically. Faith as such is celebrated, if in it an unfeigned look upward to God shines forth, and love extends itself to the universe, to man ennobled through service, to transfigured existence and noble fulfillment of purpose.

Misconceptions about the genuineness and high-mindedness of

these convictions are to be categorically rejected, and generally
would not deserve notice if they had been advanced merely in a
frivolous manner by the spiteful. The experience of the living effect of such passages as those, perhaps, in the fifth movement of
the Third would certainly not have permitted such misinterpretations to arise. It is regrettable that parts of works by such a pro-
foundly gifted artistic nature as Mahler's could be exposed to such
constructions. Irony makes itself felt here and there in symphonic
passages, but never in those devoted to the divine or to the love of
one's fellow men. The ironical and satirical passages must be distinguished from the humorous ones. Nothing is frivolous. The
deep moral seriousness of the artist holds sway over everything –
he is always in the service of the strictest religion of art. Everything is ennobled by a purifying ethos. In the movement from the
Third mentioned above, 'the angels' (according to another
marking 'the morning bells') relate a legend that is captured in
tones with the purest naivety of spirit; an almost childlike faith is
expressed in the musical setting of this 'children's heaven without
suffering and sin' (Wilhelm Kienzl's designation).[57] Where the
poem combines faith and humor, as in the final movement of the
Fourth, the composer makes use of humor on the basis of profound seriousness (as is characteristic of genuine, liberating
humor) and, in addition, presents an untroubled musical conception of faith in paradise, which indeed might not, in Mahler's
view, correspond to the highest conception of the eternal. To
avoid any misunderstanding, Mahler expressly dictates for the
voice part: 'With a childlike, bright expression, absolutely without
parody!' The trumpets and horns of the 'great summons' in the
closing part of the Second resound like a signal for the elevation of
the spirit into eternal spheres: the chorale that follows, 'Auferstehen, ja auferstehen' (after words of Klopstock), is sounded with
a matchless emotional depth. He who with such fervor sings the
words 'I am from God and wish to return to God, dear God will
give a light, will light me a way into the eternally blessed life' (in
the fourth movement of the Second), has seen and experienced
the essence of the religion that is anchored on the firm foundation
of love of one's fellow men: 'That which you have loved is yours'
[as Mahler says in the finale of the Second]. Only in this way could
Mahler raise himself up to the singer of joy greeted by the Italian
Alfredo Casella: 'Mahler is the only musician who has grasped the

true import of the *Ode to Joy*.[58] The Frenchman William Ritter,
a strictly-orthodox Catholic, apostrophizes Mahler with the words:
'You are the true *Ode to Joy*'.[59] Now, fortunately, in the rich
gallery of music history, we have other artists who have in similar
fashion fulfilled this mission. But that Mahler certainly does not
stand in the last rank is undeniable. No one who ever came into
close contact with his fascinating personality, or who approaches
his art with impartiality, can doubt the honesty of his convictions
or the candor of his nature. Just as (at the time of his activity in
Vienna) his intellect penetrated into the works of Kant, his heart
kept its naive belief in fairy-tales and in a visionary fairy-tale bliss,
and he saw with a transfigured artist's view into the heaven that
opened itself to him. With the childlike spirit of the folk song he
was able to raise himself to that point where only imagination and
faith, not reason, escort one. A deep longing – for the infinite –
runs through almost all of his works, and the finite does not
disrupt the seer's view. He performs his devotions in nature and
prays in sounds. A yearning for nature stands out here and there,
such as that which fills the culture-weary wanderer of the world of
our time. Schiller characterizes a poet such as this, who seeks
nature, as 'sentimental', and the poet who is himself nature, as
'naive'. In Mahler the naive and the sentimental alternate – his
nature was complex and shows contrasts that were heightened by
his temperament. Hence cross contrasts also appear in his art.

At many places in his scores the marking 'like a nature sound' is
found. Mahler does not describe nature pictures and happenings
externally, but sets them to music as experiences; their artistic re-
creation is, as Beethoven put it, 'more the expression of feelings
than painting'. The motives are fashioned in accordance with
strict musical style principles and by this means are raised to
musical images of experiences. In external manner Mahler is not a
programmatic composer; he does not intend to re-create any real
program and withdraws ever further from such endeavors, which
could lure the master of technique onto a path that would take
him away from his most individual sphere of work. Since his title
vignettes were exposed to misinterpretations, he removed those
that the First and Third Symphonies in their entirety had
received, and also those of the individual movements of the Third,
just as Robert Schumann had done in connection with the fourth
movement of his E-flat major symphony, giving as his reason: 'one

should not show people one's heart; a more general impression of
the work of art is better for them, for then at least they make no
topsy-turvy comparisons'. Mahler's headings, which were not
added to the published scores but were given only by way of expli-
cation in the program books of the first performances, had from
the first no more than a generally indicative character and were
not intended in any way to limit the imagination of the listener.
They were entrance keys, which could open the way into the
edifice, and which at its conception possibly gave wings to the
imagination of the creator, without determining the shaping of
the work. The texts that were added to individual parts were not
from the first determinative for the mood, the expressive content,
of the pieces or movements in question, but only seemed welcome
as associative partners of the music. 'When I plan a large musical
painting I always arrive at the point where I must draw on the
word as the bearer of my musical idea',[60] he wrote to Arthur Seidl
in 1897. He did not always arrive at this point; on the contrary,
after the Fourth he continually renounced the use of words to accompany his music (for this is the true, real relationship in
Mahler's symphonies, not the use of music to accompany words):
only in the Eighth Symphony, in which he worked out the basic
plan of the Second in an entirely new manner, did he have recourse, in both its parts, to texts. In spite of its outward appearance as a cantata, it is a symphony in name and in inner character. The formal element is co-determinative here: the first movement corresponds completely to a sonata movement, while the
second part is a synthesis of Adagio, Scherzo and Finale.[61] Liszt
undertook a similar compression in his one-movement B minor
Sonata. Just as J.S. Bach designated individual cantatas as
'Concerto', so Mahler could send this cyclic composition into the
world as a symphony, as his Eighth. To be more precise: in the
former the word 'Concerto' (an instrumental form) is only an attendant marking, for the whole definitely sprang from the soil of
the cantata; in the latter, however, the symphonic element was
pre-determinative, while the words – as important and significant
as they are – are the secondary, attendant element for the composition. Herein also lies an essential difference from Schumann's
setting of the Goethe text, the final part of *Faust,* which forms the
conclusion of his *Scenes from Faust.* In Mahler the final part of
Faust is the textual base of the second part of the symphony,

which, as was already the case earlier in Mahler's symphonies, embraces several movements. The preceding hymn, 'Veni creator spiritus', is organized and divided in complete conformity with sonata form. The form was so determinative that during the composition the artist lacked textual passages for the conclusion and subsequently drew upon the doxology – and this procedure, strange to say, also conformed to ecclesiastical custom and to liturgical usage in psalms and individual hymns.[62]

Thus the formal motive stands in the center of the entire symphonic production of Mahler, as does strophic organization in his songs. Nor did Mahler break up and destroy symphonic form; rather, he enlarged and partly reconstructed it, like Beethoven, Schubert, Bruckner and Brahms, whose works in this regard, as in general, are the ancestors of Mahler's symphonic family. The ancestry of Beethoven shows through most strongly. The influence of Schubert is noticeable in the second movement of the Second, and in the second theme of the first movement and in the trio of the Scherzo of the First. In his early works the 'modern' bearing and treatment is linked to the precedent of Bruckner, orchestrally as well as in the reminiscences of chorales and in the type of contrapuntal treatment. Specific Austrian touches make themselves lastingly felt through the use of melodies of his Moravian–Bohemian homeland (in all his works, but especially in the third movements of the Second and the Third and even in the second movement of the Ninth), and in the Scherzos, in which *Ländler* and waltzes are assimilated in transformations and syntheses (in the First as also in the Ninth etc.) Austrian military figures, as mentioned before, play a not-unimportant role.

Mahler's art is no conglomeration of these components, but a new-born creation from the artist's essential being and his own individual talent. The word 'eclecticism' has also been applied to Mahler, especially by those whose views have been formed, or, more accurately, mis-formed, by the assertions in Chamberlain's *Foundations of the Nineteenth Century* (crooked foundations, from which everything true slides off)[63] and similar literary productions. Mahler stands on the firm soil of German culture, like the masters already cited who preceded him. His Jewish lineage may perhaps explain the occasionally pronounced over-sharpening of expressive force and the fanatical exaggeration in the re-creation of his spiritual impulses. But whether this tendency can be traced back exclusively to lineage remains an open question, for it is also perceptible in thoroughly German masters. Thus Richard Wagner, who, as he 'only felt himself well, when he was beside himself', heightened expression to the extreme, to the greatest extreme. And just there is his power at its greatest, as in *Tristan.* To term Mahler a follower of Berlioz is also stylistically a bad mistake, both with regard to the nature of Mahler's voice-leading and with regard to his aesthetic attitude; for just as he was far-removed from the programmatic, he never considered sonority an end in itself and used it merely as a means. To be sure, Mahler did learn from this master of sound. That he resembles Berlioz in coloristic mastery is a phenomenon that results from the expressive power of Mahler's art and from the master's sense of sonority. Like every true art, that of Mahler directs itself to all musically civilized cultures and also has the power gradually to conquer them. In the performances of the Allgemeiner Deutscher Musikverein,[64] in which Richard Strauss in particular, as president, and also Hermann Kretzschmar, interceded in his favor, Mahler made his first durable conquests; his first real victories he won in the Philharmonic Concerts of German Prague;[65] in Munich, Mannheim, Graz and Amsterdam, as well as other cities, he achieved lasting successes; in Vienna he later gained a strong community of admirers. In the two first-named cities Mahler festivals were arranged. 'The genius of Gustav Mahler is representative of the great traditions of German music,' says Gerhart Hauptmann, and 'He has the daemonic character and passionate ethical quality of German masters.'[66] 'Certainly there is no German musician who lives with a keener awareness', the Graz writer on music, Ernst Decsey, cries emphatically.[67] It is certain that Mahler's melodic idiom grew from the soil of the folk music of his homeland, that his thematic treatment was formed on the procedures of the masters named above, that his songs already reveal in the handling of language the most intimate connection between the composer and the poet and, in the poems written and set to music by him, show the German feeling for the inseparable unity of language and music. Moreover, one who could perform Wagner, Beethoven, Mozart, Lortzing and others with the stylistic purity displayed by Mahler, and this for the most part without external models but from within himself, from intuition, is a true German artist; like every universal master, he possessed the ability to enter also into the spirit of other stylistic paths.

In conducting his own works and those of others, the character

of the conductor and the work of art conducted both manifested
themselves. He buried himself in the work to be performed, and it
drew him in, so that he completely surrendered to it. Subject and
object became one. While he re-created the work of art, he led
those working with him and guided by him, his companions, with
an irresistible power of suggestion, and drew them over to his conception. He allowed his co-workers just as much freedom as was
possible at any time without damaging an integrated performance. He extracted the utmost capacity for work from the players
and placed them all in the service of the composition. At the same
time he subjugated them to his will and with a general's look assigned the divisions of his troops in accordance with his master
plan, which was based on the music itself and was ordered in accordance with the situation and the forces at hand. In rehearsals
one could observe how, step by step, the ground was taken and
mastered, how, in the careful polishing of the smallest details, his
view was directed to the unity of the whole. Sometimes he gives a
comparative explanation, sometimes with throat and lips, suggesting a wind instrument or fiddle, sings a motive or passage,
with arm and hand indicates the lines, the type of movement,
stabs the air, in a crescendo grows into a giant, in a decrescendo
shrinks into a dwarf, with his looks, his threatening brows, the
pleading corners of his mouth, his furrowed forehead, entices the
greatest intimacy and the greatest tension from *pppp* all the way
to *ffff*. He enlivens with humorous words, censures in a sarcastic
manner – but always to spur the players and singers on to 'new
deeds'. He tells an anecdote that is intended to revivify the
imagination. The softest middle-voice in a movement in many
parts he hears and corrects if it sounds untrue; in the midst of a
roaring attack he rejects the sound of an instrument that has not
begun properly; in a large chorus notes a singer who intones an
octave too low, in the *tutti* a violinist who plays the right note but
does so on an unsuitable string. From orchestras expressly assembled, or, more accurately, thrown together, for individual
performances of his symphonies and other works, he created
homogeneous instrumental bodies in a few rehearsals. In piano rehearsals for opera and concert he controlled the instrument with
whose sounds he accompanied the singers in a consummate
manner. He was able to give the illusion of the orchestra and at

the same time held himself within the required limits in relation to the vocal parts. In chamber ensembles he proved himself a sensitive companion of his partners – here he sketched with delicate lines within the framework of the miniature picture. He had a special predilection for playing chamber music. As a *Lieder* accompanist he was able to adapt himself to the singer and at the same time lead him without allowing his guidance to be felt. In separate wind or string rehearsals he sought to maintain the balance of sound necessary in the entire orchestra and yet at the same time permit each player to feel himself a soloist.

As he is totally absorbed – to the last fiber – in the work of art, so he expects the same from his co-workers. He will not relent until everything is achieved that seems achievable to him. He demands the continuation, repetition and augmentation of the rehearsals. Here he hits the most substantial resistance – to the musicians, earning a livelihood is of equal importance, excessive exertion disagreeable. To most men – and especially to certain musicians – it seems an unpardonable transgression to become uncomfortable. As a result, in Vienna conflicts developed – manifesting themselves not in noisy opposition, but in a growing quiet resentment, which accumulated and subsequently relieved itself through ostracism. Works which, although they did not at first touch Mahler sympathetically, he accepted for performance, either because he gradually felt closer to them, as was the case for example with Pfitzner's *Die Rose vom Liebesgarten,* or because, induced by various circumstances, he had to bring himself around to them – which indeed happened only exceptionally – such works he treated with the same attentiveness and the same dedication as works that were flesh of his flesh, spirit of his spirit, regardless of whether he or others had created them. In the realm of art he hated nothing more than the mechanical – not to be confused with the mechanical tools of the musician or the 'golden mechanics' of art in creation and re-creation. He could grow angry like the youth in *Prometheus Unbound.*[68]

> Mechanics are they, who for base reward,
> Aping their great forbears, sham art!
> Does the deep yearning glow in their breasts,
> The pain-rich impulse toward their Goddess?
> They do not believe in their own work,

Hence will never be believed!
They cannot move others, for they themselves
Are not moved!

These words of Lipiner were almost a motto for the activity of his friend Mahler. He could move others, because he was himself deeply moved, in the holy, sacrificial service of his art.

When the little man with the lively movements approached the conductor's desk, silence fell. With friendly, clear and sympathetic voice he greeted the musicians, who, conjured by his look, surrendered themselves to his guiding will as soon as he raised his baton. Seriousness and holy zeal speak from his features, his shining eyes spread light and clarity, looking down as if lost in reverie in mystical passages; his energetic will manifests itself in his vigorous chin as well as in the animated nostrils of his sharply incised nose and in his high forehead, in which furrows appear as soon as doubt and anger arise. On the other hand a gentle smile can speak from his delicate, thin lips. Considering everything, and superior to everything, he indulged himself freely in his bodily motions, frequently to the point of grotesqueness, with nervous twitching and foot-stamping. Yet in riper years his movements became increasingly concentrated. The arms seem to want to satisfy themselves with the necessary indication of time and tempo, eyes and expression bore into the attentively upturned faces, wrist and fingertips accomplish more now than arms and feet earlier. Mahler's conducting became more and more spiritualized, and his will communicated itself as if in electrical discharges, which remained invisible to the eyes of the listeners. Mahler's work in conducting and composing became constantly more intense. This process reveals itself especially in the stylistic makeup of his works. The arches of his melodies remain broadly extended, but the motivic organization becomes more and more complex, the web of the parts becomes increasingly intricate and at times is compressed into an almost impenetrable thicket. The moods are drawn out of the most hidden recesses of his soul, and he seeks to capture all his impulses and aspirations in ever-growing intertwinings. Perhaps he went too far in this regard. Nevertheless in this respect he was also one of the stylistic leaders of his time, a genuine and legitimate representative of the 'modern' in the last decade of the previous century and the first decade of our own. He was able to expand with increasing freedom and

yet held fast to inherited forms. He increased the means, enriched
the color, intensified the expression, multiplied the harmonic
stimuli, but nevertheless remained more or less on a diatonic
foundation, even though he often combined harmonic and non-
harmonic notes simultaneously, with the boldest use of appog-
giaturas (often piled up), anticipations and passing notes. Within
his diatonic idiom (so intended, but not absolutely), augmented
and diminished intervals and cross-relations of all kinds are used,
with the greatest possible avoidance of pure chromatic harmony
but with the introduction of chromatic passages as a coloristic
means of intensifying sound. Major and minor are associated as
though in one and the same basic key; he joins them together
successively and simultaneously. The movement from major to
minor in the same chord (the tonic and dominant notes retained,
the major third shifting to the minor) is almost a symbol for joy
and sorrow, which in life so quickly and directly succeed one
another, a sonorous reflection of the optimistic and pessimis-
tic conceptions of life that stand out in the works of the musical
poet Mahler, without a tendency to favor one or the other exclusively. Sometimes a sudden shift from minor to major appears, as
in the second movement of the Fourth (see Example 1):

Example 1. Fourth Symphony, 2nd movement, mm. 142-7

Sometimes the major–minor progression forms the *Leitmotiv* of an entire symphony (the Sixth, and taken up again in the second movement of the Seventh, see Examples 2 and 3):

Example 2. Sixth Symphony, 1st movement, mm. 59-60

Example 3. Seventh Symphony, 2nd movement, mm. 28-9

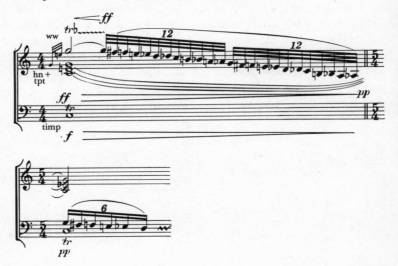

It had already been sounded in the first movement of the Second, and is of particular significance in *Das Lied von der Erde* (first, second and last movement, 'Abschied', which hovers between minor and major). Then occasionally they are combined, just as altogether different keys are sounded simultaneously - an essential characteristic of the style of the masters of our time. Harmonic intensifications and relaxations are achieved with new means, which, like the [contrapuntal] combinations that build up

through the joining of parts, and also the rhythmic intensifications and abatements in general, merit detailed description. In all
of these matters he distinguishes himself from his contemporaries
and forms a stylistic model for others. He merges keys (even sharp
and flat keys), the harmonic and melodic minor scales, major and
minor, but here also only when something uncommon is to be
expressed, when the individual melodic lines that are brought
together logically justify such harmonic treatment. Keys follow
one another directly in a tonal reflection of surprise, in especially
striking ways in the Scherzo of the Fifth (B-flat major – D major),
in the first movement of the Sixth (E minor – C major) and in
other works. In individual songs and symphonies he does not close
in the key in which he had begun; he does this not for the sake of
low humor, nor because of any insufficiency in his powers of
organization, but for psychological reasons, as is already apparent
in 'Ging heut' Morgen über's Feld' and 'Die zwei blauen Augen
von meinem Schatz' in the *Lieder eines fahrenden Gesellen*. The
wanderer moves in a direction that departs from the one originally
taken; the eyes of his beloved lead him far away. Likewise in the
cycle of movements in the symphonies, with profound significance
the Fifth begins in C-sharp minor, ends in D major, the Seventh,
B minor – C major, the Ninth, D major – D-flat major, a rise in
the former works, an especially meaningful fall in the latter, in
the closing movement of which the musical poet, as it were, takes
his leave. Everything grows out of inner need, out of impulse, not
from a passion to provoke, and not with the intention of dazzling.
Such reproaches were raised by opponents who, following a
Wagnerian formula, suspect a passion for effect in others.

The rhythmic formations become increasingly varied both in
the individual melodic lines, through occasional quick meter
changes, and in the combination of several melodies, which here
and there, even disregarding regulated part-writing, buffet one
another in a heterophonic manner – like the opposing forces in
life, the antitheses in nature; for (as Goethe says) everything is in
nature, the harsh, the gentle, the charming and frightful, the
powerless and the all-powerful. One could add, the beautiful and
the ugly. The greatest harshness is found re-created in the symphonies, as in the second movement of the Sixth. Humor often
builds up into the savage, the grotesque (as in the second movement[69] of the Fifth).

Melodic passages now and then grate against one another in seconds or sevenths or ninths, either to preserve the individual flow of the parts, which strike harshly against one another in space, or in a pitiless reproduction of the pitilessness of life, the cacophonies of the inner life. Sometimes the parts move in fourths in the manner of the old Netherlanders, or in modern coloristic service for the reciprocal reinforcement of sound. Passages in fifths also serve this purpose, or parallel fifths and octaves show an archaizing character and are handled like *organum,* in the fashion of 'primitive' musical treatment at the beginning of the art; then, at times they have an almost rustic character, in a countrified style (as was already customary in the villanellas of the seventeenth century), which is particularly drastic in the third movement of the Third (see Example 4):

Example 4. Third Symphony, 3rd movement, mm. 30-3

The naivety of such voice-leading, which goes back to time-honored church practices, can accompany the musical poetry into higher regions, as in the Resurrection Chorus of the Second (see Example 5), in the fourth movement of the Fourth ('St Peter im Himmel sieht zu', see Example 6) and in very important passages in the Fifth and Eighth.

Example 5. Second Symphony, Resurrection Chorus, mm. 482-6

Example 6. Fourth Symphony, 4th movement, mm. 36-8

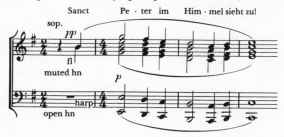

Mahler shows a conspicuous predilection for basing both simple and complex sections on upper, lower or middle pedal-points. He makes use of the possibility of introducing sustained voices in all registers with an abundance equaled by few masters. Whole sections are tonally supported in this fashion, like the trio of the second movement of the Second (see Example 7) and the beginning of the second movement of the Eighth, where E-flat^3 sounds for 164 measures in the first violins while the other stringed instruments remain firmly fixed on one motive – a deeply symbolic, uncanny outline of the anchoritic mood expressed there (see Example 8).

Example 7. Second Symphony, 2nd movement, mm. 39-41

Example 8. Eighth Symphony, 2nd movement, mm. 1-6

Pedal-point and ostinato merge imperceptibly into one another: thus the 'fixed' note in the third movement of the Second fluctuates between E and E-flat;[70] basses murmur quasi-ostinato notes that are almost or actually motives in the first movement of the Second (see Example 9), in the fifth movement of the Third (see Example 10), in the second movement of the Sixth (see Example 11):

Example 9. Second Symphony, 1st movement, mm. 80, 91

Example 10. Third Symphony, 5th movement, mm. 1-4

Example 11. Sixth Symphony, 2nd movement, mm. 1-6

Or a chord, like a stubborn person, insists with stupid, foolish obstinacy on its right to sound, as if for its own amusement – as in life – untroubled about what arises from it harmonically. See, for example, the principal theme of the first movement of the

Seventh, with the rhythmically ordered E minor harmony in the two-line octave (Example 12):

Example 12. Seventh Symphony, 1st movement, mm. 50-4

A note then gradually begins to move. The sustained note is dissolved in the rhythmic lower parts, circumscribed in ornaments and melismas, converted into motives that are repeated with a persistence that points to Beethoven, and was also especially popular in masterworks of the seventeenth century, worked out, of course, in a different manner, and proceeding from different psychic motives. Polyphonic writing infiltrates his style with increasing importance for structure as a whole. His accomplishments in this regard become extraordinary from the Fifth on. He employs canons only rarely, as in the second movement of the Fifth (an episode between woodwinds and 'cellos, see Example 13):

Example 13. Fifth Symphony, 2nd movement, mm. 288-95

Instead he makes use of fugal work in combination with sonata or rondo structure in the manner of late Beethoven, as in the third movement of the Second, in the last movement of the Fifth (triple fugue), in the development of the first movement of the Eighth (double fugue) and in the third movement of the Ninth (with the inscription in the manuscript 'to my brothers in Apollo'). In the second movement of the Second he already uses a smoothly unfolding violoncello melody, a sweet tune, as counterpoint to the first theme (in double counterpoint, see Example 14):

Example 14. Second Symphony, 2nd movement, mm. 93-6

In the first movement, the second half of the first theme makes its first appearance as a counterpoint (see Example 15):

Example 15. Second Symphony, 1st movement, mm. 18-22

But the artifices increase especially in the Fifth, Sixth and Seventh, in the first movement of which the principal theme appears in similar and contrary motion in three-fold stretto (see Example 16):

Example 16. Seventh Symphony, 1st movement, mm. 378-81

Double and triple augmentation and diminution and many similar techniques appear repeatedly. Variations in the true sense, as an independent form, are not favored; they are introduced in a free realization in the third movement of the Fourth through metamorphoses of the principal melody. On the other hand, the varying of themes is one of the principal means of construction and becomes increasingly diverse from the time of the Fifth on. His teachers may not have stressed it enough. The more he became absorbed in symphonic work, the more he penetrated into thematic variation, and the greater his skill grew.

A precious gem in just this connection is *Das Lied von der Erde,*

which is also built on a symphonic foundation. Here he reduces
the themes to their basic elements (see Example 20, p. 66 below)
and from these he forms new themes and distributes the material
in all the parts. His special attention is directed to clear organization. As broadly as he may extend his arches – the themes themselves are extended in a previously-unheard-of manner (cf. my
Der Stil in der Musik) – he directs equal attention to the logic of
the expansion. The rise and fall of the themes is of the most impressive plasticity. One frequently sees themes come into being –
from introductory motives they are developed, born, before one's
eyes and ears, as in the first movements of the Third and Sixth
and in the final movement of the latter. Then they are diminished, contracted and expanded again; individual themes stand in
closer or more distant degrees of relationship to one another, or
parts of them are similar (as in the second movement of the Fifth).
They are combined with one another, like the principal and
second themes in the first movement of the Seventh. Frequently
the auxiliary ideas accumulate in a way that confuses even the at-
tentive and practiced listener, as in the Scherzo of the Fifth, and,
in almost a Babylonian-tower architectural style, in the Finale of
the Sixth. In other cases he subsequently eliminates re-entries of
passages that seem unnecessary to him, as in the second movement
of the Second. In the Finale of the Seventh the important themes
are found united within a few measures, likewise in the recapitulation of the first movement of the Fifth. The themes are so forcibly,
so sharply, profiled that their physiognomy remains recognizable
even beneath the mummeries of the variations. As in every
original artist, certain idioms appear: they may be traced from
the first symphony and also from the first song – Mahleresque
turns that are especially apparent in the Fifth and Sixth, at the
time when Mahler had completely formed his own individual style
– and prove irrefutably that this master is no eclectic. Naturally
he does not limit himself to the introduction of material only in
the exposition, but also occasionally brings in new themes in the
further course of the work. Beethoven had brought in a new
theme in the development of the first movement of the 'Eroica',[71]
and Mahler does the same in the first movement of the Second.
Following the example of the great master, in Mahler's works the
climax is contained within the development section. In the recapitulation the themes are often presented in a different

sequence; the material is shaped in accordance with the processes of the spiritual stimuli without departing from the principal requirements, the foundation pillars, of the respective forms. Even where free episodes, improvisatory creations, are inserted in an apparently loose manner, they are thoroughly incorporated into the organism of the regular form. In the Sixth, which yields to the tragic conception of life in an almost luxurious manner, the exigencies of strict formal treatment were so fully observed that they acted in a formally determinative manner even on the inner course of the work; outwardly they are recognizable through the otherwise no-longer-customary repetition of the exposition of the first movement.

In addition to the balanced proportions of the formal structure and the melodic lines, the perspective of the orchestration serves as an auxiliary means of achieving clarity and forcefulness. As powerful as the orchestration may seem, it never effaces the distinctness of the groupings. 'The plasticity of Mahler's art of instrumentation is absolutely exemplary', says Richard Strauss,[72] certainly the most well-qualified judge of coloristic treatment. The ideas and their manner of expression are converted into sound-images. The ideas are primary, the coloring secondary, which is the healthy relationship. At the same time the association of the timbres of certain instruments with individual themes at the very time of their creation is not ruled out. Mahler confessed that he often found it difficult to discover orchestration that was suitable, even though he easily could have manufactured it. Thus even after its publication the Fifth was subjected to a thorough re-instrumentation, which was partly related in this case to the transformation of his style from the Fourth to the Fifth. On the palette of his orchestra all the colors, all the mixtures of colors, of the modern style are to be found, and he increased them in a not-insignificant manner.

As in Classic and Romantic times the usual string and wind instruments form the basic and principal means, but they are increased (individual groups are doubled or tripled) and supplemented with new ones and subdivided into still more parts, in a manner similar to many of his contemporaries. The E-flat clarinet, with its piercing timbre, already utilized by Berlioz, is taken over from the military orchestra. Celesta, guitar and mandolin had already been used by others, but by no one in a manner more distinctive than Mahler's. Piano and harmonium are introduced to reconcile and unite sonorities. Here and there the solo violin is re-tuned, as was done not infrequently in the seventeenth century and by individual virtuosos in later times, especially Paganini. The sound of the organ in the Second and the Eighth is not ephemeral in the [symphonic] literature; it appears in these works of Mahler at the bidding of the poetic mood. Mahler differentiates the percussion instruments in an unsuspected manner and in this respect far outdoes even Berlioz. Timpani, bass drum, snare drum, cymbals, gong, tambourine, slapstick and xylophone are used; the twig brush had already been employed by Mozart. Mahler teaches these instruments a previously unknown language; with them he fills in general pauses and divides them in a rhythmic manner; he makes the percussion serviceable for the purpose of transition. They are employed as sonorous auxiliaries and as attendant phenomena of psychic impulses and impressions, in the first movement of the Third, for example, as a suggestion of a spectral apparition. Twice (at different places) in the Finale of the Sixth a hammer stroke vibrates deeply (according to the instructions 're-sounding briefly, dully, powerfully without a metallic quality'),[73] both to reinforce the stroke of the orchestra and to suggest the dull stroke of fate. Chimes ring as a token of celestial life or as if for the accompaniment of occurrences in an animate nature, as in the fifth movement of the Third and in the first movements of the Fifth and Eighth. They also sound from the mouths of children, as if struck by angels – as heavenly bells (see Example 10, p. 52 above). Such imitations of the voices of bells are already found in Medieval compositions and also during the golden age of a-cappella music. In the Sixth the cowbells do not sound for the purpose of tone-painting, i.e. perhaps to suggest a herd of cows or sheep. With them Mahler wished, as he explained, 'only to characterize an earthly noise, fading away in the farthest distance, which the lonely one on the mountain peak overhears as a symbol of the greatest isolation'.[74] They occur again in the second movement of the Seventh. Such sound-effects, and others similar to them, are exceptional in the total sonority of his works. Even a great master of color makes experiments that do not always succeed. But if he perceived a mistake or deficiency he made changes until what was to be said communicated itself clearly and comprehensibly in the sound-image. The use of unaccustomed re-

gisters of individual woodwind and brass instruments and the temporary direction that they are to be played with the bells held
high, or that the player is to stand up, serve the same purpose.
Who can argue that these practices reflect an excessive striving for
clarification? From the fact that he requires neither trombones
nor tubas in the Fourth, one can easily perceive that Mahler's
demands do not grow out of a mania for color. In the Adagietto of
the Fifth only strings and harp are employed. The orchestration
of his songs also shows how selective he was in introducing
timbres, sometimes requiring more, sometimes fewer. Yet the
criticism that his instrumentation is occasionally overloaded, even
in comparison with Wagnerian scores, especially that of *Tristan,*
has been raised by knowledgeable persons. Who is right? Everything has its appropriate style; if it only says and means something, then one must acknowledge it and not attempt to transform
it into another style. One's view must be kept on the object, and
the view changes in any case with each viewer or listener. The
most intrinsic life-tissue of music is, and remains, the melodic element. In observing this fundamental tenet Mahler differs considerably from many of his 'brothers in Apollo' who were active
around him or who presume to continue his artistic practice.
Mahler's tunes always give evidence of character and have a convincing effect for those who come to them in order to believe.
They are not always refined, for he wants the vulgar, which he
utilizes as an antithesis. He also lets the common people speak and
strikes up rustic tunes, like Bruckner before him. Such tunes are
seldom lacking in originality, especially when he delineates Philis-
tinism, the common pair of lovers in the alley, the amorous
postilion, the 'tramp' who accompanies the town music (a Viennese speciality), ambles down the road and idles away precious
time. The symphonic composer can reproduce these trivialities if,
as previously stated, they are embedded in the foundation of a
serious conception of life. In his 'Pastoral' Beethoven has depicted
the village musicians, how their tune drowsily comes to a stand-
still, and, frightened, they join in again. As it was then 'local
custom' in Hinterbrühl, in Gaaden (where he wished to retire),
Beethoven set and ordered it artistically. Mahler the tone-painter
[*Maler*] of 'vanity fair' found and gathered other strains in the
market-place of life. In a century will they also sound as ennobled
as the strains of Beethoven's village inn today? Melodically weak,

for example, are the second theme of the first movement of the Sixth and some themes of the Ninth, yet the first theme of the latter symphony belongs among his most beautiful notions. Mahler's melodic writing hovers between folkish traits and the highest artistic development. In the third movement of the First the indication 'simply and plainly like a folk song' appears. With it he also wishes to suggest the naturalness of the execution. Nature songs are brought over into the terrain of modern art, either through the manipulation of individual notes, as is perhaps still the case in the second movement of the Sixth (see Example 11, p. 52 above), or through a setting that gives the kernel an entirely new covering. In Austrian country songs one finds leaps of sevenths which, on the individual soil of Mahler's constantly-transformed melodic style, have grown into his favorite leaps of ninths. The so-called chorales in Mahler's symphonies often belong rather to the mood-sphere of the chorale, and are individual tunes in the melodic style of the artist. When his technique achieved mastery of motivic synthesis (from the Fifth on), he trod new musical ground, as distinctive as his language may have been in each individual earlier work. This is the natural process in every artist who has become 'his own follower', as Schubert said when someone asked him whether he was a follower of Mozart or Beethoven. In the gradual struggle for the full realization of his individuality, Mahler's manner of expression becomes an original language. In every artist with his own physiognomy, this process is necessary and organic.

If Mahler's youthful works were preserved, if with pitiless self-criticism he had not destroyed [almost] everything that he had written up to about 1882 (chamber music, the operas *Herzog Ernst von Schwaben, Die Argonauten, Rübezahl,* various orchestral works, among them a 'Nordic' suite or symphony), one could document and describe the first period of his development.[75] *Das klagende Lied,* composed at the age of eighteen to twenty years, in 1892-3 underwent a remodeling that resulted in the omission of the first part; further revisions in the instrumentation were undertaken in 1898.[76] It is no song: it was originally thought of as a fable for the stage,[77] and was realized as a cantata study. The text was written by Mahler after a fairy tale told by Bechstein, and the poetry seems to me more animated than the music, which makes not-inconsiderable demands on soloists, chorus and large orchestra. The music hovers between concert and theater and cannot disavow its original disposition for the latter. In addition to individual melodic turns it shows other original features: quick key-changes (C-sharp minor – C major), the use of major seventh chords, and the rapid alternation of *fff* and *ppp*. Since in addition to this work only some songs that appeared under the title of *Jugendliedern* (1880-3?; published 1892)[78] are preserved from his youthful period, the historian cannot discuss the first period, although he must take it for granted that it exists. Of these songs, one ('Frühlingsmorgen') leans on Schumann, another ('Hans und Grethe') stands on the soil of folk song. After considering the foregoing creations, two periods must be distinguished in the subsequent works, as also recognized by Bruno Walter:[79] the first of these style-periods (i.e. the second in the entire domain of Mahler's creations) embraces the time from 1883 to 1900. Four symphonies originated in it as well as the especially-characteristic *Lieder eines fahrenden Gesellen* (1884-5, texts also written by him) and the songs from *Des Knaben Wunderhorn* (*c*. 1887/8-1901). Mahler had become acquainted with the latter collection only at the age of twenty-eight,[80] but in his poetic longing had divined their spirit well before then (already in the poetry of *Das klagende Lied*). For, as Goethe says, the poet knows the world through anticipation. This second sight plays a singular role in Mahler's life: thus he wrote the *Kindertotenlieder* before he had lost his beloved first-born daughter. Before the angel of death had grazed him he composed the concluding movement of *Das Lied von der Erde* and the Ninth as a farewell to life.[81] In his songs he first achieved his full individuality in just this second period: 'Revelge' and 'Der schildwache Nachtlied' are the most individual Mahler, the 'genuine' Mahler, I might say, if this designation might not result in misinterpretation in connection with other works. They are as distinctly original as, in the following period, 'Ich bin der Welt abhanden gekommen', 'Um Mitternacht', the *Kindertotenlieder* (the Rückert songs in general) and *Das Lied von der Erde,* the summit of the song pyramid. From the *Klagende Lied* to the last-named work an immense journey into a completely new land is traversed. In addition to the Rückert songs and *Das Lied von der Erde* the later symphonies (Fifth to Ninth) also belong to this third creative period. The Italian Casella (living in Paris) and the Frenchman

William Ritter would like to begin a new period with the Ninth.[82] I can see no plausible reason for this. The stylistic workmanship is not different, only the manner of realization and organization that corresponds to the mood content. Mahler started with the song, chamber music and opera, and subsequently continued to cultivate only the song and the symphony. As one of the most adroit opera conductors he turned completely away from the composition of operas: for opera he became a leader in reproduction, for the symphony a pathfinder, and his works are becoming a milestone for the future. This alienation from opera composition is deeply rooted in Mahler's nature. Like few others he was a master of how operas are made but he wished to immerse himself completely in the realm of pure music. His activity as a conductor and director offered him a livelihood: he had brothers and sisters and later his own family to care for.

He was called a 'summer composer'. In the winter he usually worked out what he had drafted in the summer during the holidays. The moment he left the Opera, he belonged to himself, called 'his own tune', as Beethoven said when he turned away from opera. He created his symphonies in solitary rural seclusion. Creation was a refreshment for him. There he sang his songs, which seem like entrance ways into his symphonic structures. The former are the intimate spiritual landscapes, the latter the great spiritual murals; genre pictures stand side by side with musical representations of the cosmos. The musical spirit that animates the two types is the same and joins them into one. Just as songs of the middle period are taken over into the symphonies of the same time (the Wayfarer song 'Ging heut' Morgen über's Feld' in the first movement of the First, returning motivically in the third and fourth movements, 'Des Antonius von Padua Fischpredigt' in the third movement of the Second, 'Der Kuckuck hat sich zu Tode gefallen' in the Scherzo of the Third), references to passages from his songs are found everywhere in the symphonies. His last song cycle 'of the earth' is – I would say – a symphony at heart, even with regard to the formal treatment of the individual parts. The Ninth is plainly the full symphonic assimilation of the musical-poetic substance contained in *Das Lied von der Erde,* the first movement in particular corresponding with 'Abschied'. While in song composition Mahler begins with strophic treatment as his foundation, he combines it with specifically musical elaboration and thus achieves structures in which the elaboration appears decisive, form-determining, especially through motivic development in the interludes. This procedure becomes apparent in the songs of the third period; at first it was connected with the example of Schumann and Brahms, and then it shows an advance in common with Hugo Wolf, Richard Strauss and others. This development would have to be investigated and demonstrated in detail. Coloristically his songs are also taken over into the orchestral sphere. Here orchestrated chamber songs have to be distinguished from true orchestral songs, the former designation used in the sense of the 'large chamber music' of the seventeenth century and the first half of the eighteenth, which was created not so much for the small chamber or the middle-class apartment as for the large princely chamber of earlier times, and is well suited to the small concert hall of our own day. I would consider the songs 'Blicke mir nicht in die Lieder', 'Ich atmet' einen linden Duft', 'Ich bin der Welt abhanden gekommen', 'Rheinlegendchen' and the *Kindertotenlieder* cycle true chamber music in spite of their coloristic drapery, the other songs as true orchestral songs intended for the large concert hall. There are twelve of them[83] in addition to *Das Lied von der Erde*. In all Mahler composed forty-two songs.[84] The designation 'symphonic songs', which Philipp Spitta employs for the songs of Brahms, is applicable in the higher sense [of the word 'symphonic'] to the songs of Mahler. They embrace nature, the world of children and adults in the most diverse moods of love, profane and sacred, the most complete devotion descending by degrees to resignation, which achieves expression in the most luminous manner in the incomparable 'Ich bin der Welt abhanden gekommen'. In individual songs parodistic turns are found, expressly so designated in 'Aus! Aus!', where the soldier takes leave of his beloved (in a 'bold march tempo') and she suggests in her answers that both will console themselves somehow. A banal burlesque of a similar type appears in the dialogue between hussar and maiden in 'Trost im Unglück'. Distinctive kinds of markings are found in both the songs and symphonies, but especially in the latter: among others, 'with parody' in the third movement of the First, to characterize the image of the woodland animals accompanying the funeral procession of the hunter, a funeral march that makes use of the student canon 'Bruder Martin'. In the symphonies the directions are intensified to an extreme degree; for example, 'with great wildness' (fourth movement of the First), 'with great vehemence' (in the second movement of the Fifth), 'with raw power' and 'as if whipped' in the Sixth. In performance these passages must not be torn from the framework of the whole; the composer does not do so in his formal treatment. In the songs everything is ordered on the basic scaffolding of the textual pattern. Here of course he permits himself many alterations – for the sake of specific musical points. When, most exceptionally, there is a departure in the declamation, as perhaps in 'Urlicht' (fourth movement of the Second) at the word 'abweisen', it grows out of the musical context in a natural, almost compulsory, manner (see Example 17).

Example 17. Second Symphony, 4th movement, mm. 44-7

If he omits strophes in through-composed songs in many stanzas, he does so either in deference to economy of musical structure or with a view to the unfitness, the unsuitableness, of the words in question. When he inserts words, sentences or verses, as for example in the Resurrection Song of Klopstock (in the closing movement of the Second), the musical train of thought requires it, or it is the realization of a poetic demand of the composer. Occasionally he also telescopes two texts in one song, as in 'Wer hat dies Liedlein erdacht?' or in the closing number of *Das Lied von der Erde* – in this fashion an entirely new mood picture is created, a new off-spring of the word- and sound-poet Mahler, a fusion of the two texts. Through the exceptional repetition of textual passages the musical passage gains in intensity. Pure joy in singing breaks out in melismas, as in 'Wer hat dies Liedlein erdacht?' – a stream of coloraturas that sweeps one along with it (see Example 18).

Example 18. 'Wer hat dies Liedlein erdacht?', mm. 33-46

From the 428 poems that Rückert wrote under the impact of the death of his children, Mahler chooses five and creates a cycle the

Example. 19. Kindertotenlieder, 'In diesem Wetter, in diesem Braus', mm. 119-24

Haus,   wie   in   der   Mut - ter   Haus!

mood of which unites deeply moving expression with the most exalted and refined bearing. He ends with a melody that is rhythmically reminiscent of a lullaby – the children rest in the earth as if lulled by their mother. The solace softens the unspeakable pain, which is in fact unappeasable (see Example 19). More unified, still more concentrated, is the cycle *Das Lied von der Erde,* in spite of opposing moods that clash antithetically with one another. Only the most consummate mastery of music by an artist can achieve this power of concentration. The six songs are based on a fundamental motive ($a^2\ g^2\ e^2$)[85] the notes of which appear in all possible variants, in transformations in normal, inverted and retrograde order (see Example 20).

Example 20. Das Lied von der Erde

a   1st movement, mm. 5-9

b   2nd movement, mm. 3-6

c   3rd movement, mm. 3-6

d   4th movement, mm. 8-13

e   5th movement, mm. 1-2

f   6th movement, mm. 77-80

Die Blu-men   bla - sen   im Däm-mer - schein,

g   6th movement, mm. 167-72

Optimism and pessimism clash harshly with one another in space.
The former is particularly apparent in no. 3 'Von der Jugend' and
no. 4 'Von der Schönheit', the motives of which are closely connected, the latter particularly in no. 2 'Der Einsame im Herbst'
and no. 6 'Der Abschied', in a varying compound and sequence
with antecedents in no. 1 'Das Trinklied vom Jammer der Erde'
and no. 5 'Der Trunkene im Frühling'. No. 6 achieves illumination
in the consciousness that, after the death of the individual, 'everywhere the dear earth blooms and becomes green again in spring',
and attains its high point poetically and musically in the music to
the words 'O beauty, O world, drunk with eternal loving, with
life'. Everything is raised to the sublime; and this sublimity is not
disrupted even by the image of the ape (in no. 1) who crouches on
the graves in the moonlight, 'a savage spectral figure' whose apparition had already mocked Mahler the man and artist so disagreeably in life! The texts, paraphrases by Hans Bethge of
Chinese lyrics, are taken from the poetic collection *Die chinesische
Flöte* and are assembled in a free manner. The world of feeling

and mood of the four eighth-century poets, headed by Li Tai-Po,
is comprehended by the musical poet in such a way that an almost
complete interpenetration of old and new cultures is achieved.
With the means of a newly created, modern art, a union is
established across the boundaries of two arts and across a 1200-
year interval of time, as if 'old' and 'new' were completely
equivalent. The utilization of the five-note series of ancient
Chinese music in the third and fourth pieces, and the segment
taken from it in the basic motive of the cycle, is only an incidental
attendant phenomenon. The tenor voice (in three[86] songs) and the
alto or baritone (in three[87]) sing united with the subtlest timbres of
the orchestra in a new style, which seems the result of the spiritual
agitation of a time long past. This is always characteristic of
genuine works of art, which draw upon the material of old cultures, and whose universal human basic content remains the same
in different cultural periods.

Just as in this cycle and in individual songs Mahler artistically
grasps the problems of life in various ways and seeks to approach
them from the musical–poetic side, so the same content fills his
symphonies; but it is built up in larger dimensions and on exclusively musical ground, here and there with recourse to the word,
to the human voice, as a welcome elucidation of his artistic aspirations and intentions, as an association of a similar, or the same,
type of expression of mood and thought, as a completion and en-
richment of material sound in the service of the communication of
the spiritual. Then the phrases of the instrumental parts are taken
over directly by the voice parts or vice versa – there is *one* style in
which the instruments and the human voice, as an instrument,
share – as in his *Das Lied von der Erde* and also in the symphonic
movements with voices. Look, for example, at the fourth movement of the Third or the entire Eighth. I would characterize these
symphonies as cosmic art-works. Nature and life, coming into
existence and passing away, finite time and eternity, day and
night, are grasped in musical symbols. The voices of the animals
of the woods sound, the voice crying in the wilderness resounds;
the shrieks, the groaning, screaming and moaning, the rejoicing,
are audible, as are the 'huzzahs' in unfettered nature and the ex-
ultation in the open market-place and square, the quiet inti-
macies in rooms and narrow alleyways. The joys of this world and
the dreamed-of 'heavenly joys' of paradise, longed-for in faith, are

celebrated and transfigured. In the majority of his symphonies the artist struggles upward through battles and sounds of mourning to liberation from sorrow, as in the First, Second, Third, Fifth and Seventh. This liberation is of various natures: only in the First does the world-wanderer win through to a victory, to a 'triumph'. In the Fifth the striver struggles upward toward the ideal that already hovers before him, as if veiled, in the first movement; in the Seventh, radiant sunlight finally unveils itself to him. In the Second, after despair, the mourner, through yearning for God and love, attains faith, not in the sense of a creed, but rather faith in the omnipotence of love. The highest resolution of enigma is, in Mahler, pure love of God, man and nature; in the final movement of the Third the harmony of life is transfigured in devotion. The Second almost achieves fulfillment in the Eighth, where everything is directed to the 'accende lumen sensibus, infunde amorem cordibus',[88] to light and love as the core of all existence. Fourth and Sixth stand in absolute opposition to one another; in the former one finds comfort and joy in the most varied gradations and nuances, in the latter the inexorable tragedy that leads to destruction. In the Ninth, after presenting varying images of existence, the artist bids it farewell; the work closes 'dying away'. In general, in each symphony the most diverse spiritual moods achieve expression and resolve into one another, corresponding to changes in earthly life and in the weavings and workings of nature. Contrasting elements knock against one another as in the reality of existence. An almost bewildering multitude of countenances alternate with, and push against, one another. They are incorporated into the sequence of movements of the symphonic cycle, in accordance with the requirements of formal treatment and the variety needed. Frequently he changes the usual sequence (thus especially in the Ninth, where two slow movements enclose two quick ones) for the sake of the poetic, fundamental idea, which makes no real claims in a programmatic relationship but is adapted in a purely musical way and is so recognizable. Even in the darker movements, quieter moments appear to fulfill the imperative requirements of musical treatment. If one wished to follow the spiritual course of each of the nine symphonies, a detailed analysis would have to be given, which would far exceed in its dimensions what is offered here and would perhaps unnecessarily constrain those who held to it literally, fettering free interpretation. For psychical interpretation has many possibilities, almost endless varieties, and this is an advantage of musical works. Frequently the perceiver feels the work in the same way as the conceiver when he created it – even the same images or poetry pop up. But this coincidence cannot be the condition for understanding.

In the Mahler symphonies understanding is made more difficult, first of all, because, as much as each stands by itself, all belong more or less together, mutually supplement one another and even form contrasting groups, such as the Second, Third and Fourth in relation to the Fifth, Sixth and Seventh, the first group belonging more to the religious sphere, like the Eighth, the second group devoted more to the earthly. Difficulties also arise because the movements of the individual symphonies are drawn together into larger divisions and, lastly, because the movements of one and the same symphony are motivically connected. The musical-poetic significance of these connections would require special studies that would also have to deal with the fundamental questions of symphonic creation. Similar motives achieve widely varying meanings at different places in different movements and symphonies, yet still produce an inner connection. To mention one further instance (motivic connections between the Third and Fourth have been mentioned already), the Finale of the Fifth is related to that of the Seventh, even externally in the enlargement of the rondo form. The reasons for drawing individual movements of a symphony together into divisions are partly external, because of the expansion of one movement and the relative brevity of others, and partly internal, because of close inner correlations. In the Second, the second movement is to be begun only 'after a pause of at least five minutes', and then the third, fourth and fifth movements are performed with almost no interruption. In the Fifth there are three divisions: the first (the first and second movements, linked thematically) and the third (the fourth and fifth movements, likewise thematically connected) surround the second division (the Scherzo third movement). In the Seventh, three movements (the 'night music' movements) form the second part, which is enclosed by the first movement and the last (Rondo Finale) as the first and third parts. All this could be explained from the organism of the cycles. The motivic connections between individual movements of a symphony are established in various ways, as can be shown in all the symphonies.[89] Here a theme shows its true worth only in a succeeding movement – the struggling and yearning attain their goal – there a theme is struck in painful recollection of the past, then changes, alters its bearing and character and appears as a caricature or in an apotheosis. Finally, the acceptance of Mahler's symphonies is further complicated by their expansion and the time that it takes to perform them. Up to the date of the first performance of the Third, it certainly was not customary for a symphony to take up two hours (according to the estimate in the score the first movement alone takes forty-two minutes, the Finale twenty-two minutes). Each of them (with the exception of the First [and Fourth]) can fill an entire concert evening (the average time is one and one-quarter to one and one-half hours); certain ones, such as the Second, Third and Eighth, require it. What is remarkable is that even from opponents of the direction taken by Mahler – of whom there were many! – I never heard complaints of boredom. The works hold the attention of the listeners, whether friend or foe. Nevertheless, some are more approachable musical works, others are more difficult or less accessible. I would prefer not to label and differentiate them, because the more popular today may be the less frequently performed in the future and vice versa. This situation is not an unusual one in the history of music – perhaps, indeed, it is the normal one. Performance statistics thus far yield the following sequence:[90] the Fourth Symphony performed sixty-one times (since 1901), the Second forty-four times (since 1895), the First forty-four times (since 1889), the Third thirty-three times (since 1896), the Fifth twenty-two times (since 1904), the Eighth twenty-two times[91] (since 1910), the Sixth twenty-one times (since 1906), the Ninth three times (since 1913). Taking the dates of genesis and first performance into consideration, the Fourth (performed seventeen times in one year alone), the Second (eight times in one year) and the Eighth (thirteen times in one year) are especially prominent in this sequence. Thus the considerably increased demand in means in the last-named work, which concert impresarios have labeled the 'Symphony of a Thousand' (participants) – a label to which Mahler was anything but sympathetic – has not up to now hindered its dissemination. Performances of Mahler's works have extended to the following countries (the sequence based on the number of performances): Germany, Austria, Holland, France,

Switzerland, America, England, Finland, Russia, Italy, Sweden. Since 1911 *Das Lied von der Erde* has been performed fourteen times in the three first-named countries. The Eighth has been performed nineteen times in Germany, once in Austria, Holland and Switzerland. Certainly this ratio already outwardly justifies the dedication of the work 'To the German Nation'.

The works of Mahler have had to win ground for themselves step by step. At the beginning progress was very slow. As much as his muse was a child of its time, as much as the present speaks from the spirit of his art, it is still far from fashionable. His musical language is forceful, but not easily accessible in its highest and ultimate utterances. The strange mixture of the naive and sentimental creates enigmas that are not easy to unravel. On first impression his art produces attraction at one place, repulsion at another, and must be courted lovingly. The grotesque, bizarre, ironic and parodistic in individual passages and movements can be easily misunderstood. The lofty pathos, the liberating humor, the tender serenity rise above the roughnesses, which perhaps will not appear as such to a coming generation. These exalted, noble characteristics are a safeguard, a bulwark in the face of the over-intensity till now felt by many in individual passages and sections, and the hyper-subjectivism, becoming generally conspicuous in our time, which makes itself felt here and there. But at the very beginning one must not try to approach the symphonies with the aid of the piano: not infrequently what is possible orchestrally sounds strange on the keyboard. After a suitable first impression of the art-work in its appropriate sound medium, further study may be pursued in the usual way. Dissent is met with everywhere and most of all there where something new, something independent, comes to light. And Mahler was far-seeing. He built in organic union with tradition. His creations, in addition to their intrinsic value, also have meaning for the future. Beethoven, Schubert, Bruckner, Brahms in the symphonic sphere, Bach in polyphony (from the Fifth), Wagner, Liszt and Berlioz in orchestral and musical–poetic relationships, are the structural pillars of the Mahler art-work; the ground on which it is erected is that of Austrian folk music. His works range themselves beside those of his progressive contemporaries, especially beside the more programmatic direction of Richard Strauss and the more formalistic one of Max Reger. These three composers are the main supports of the music of the future. In its musical poetry Mahler's muse strives most radiantly and ideally after the sublime. Whether, and to what extent, a particular school attaches itself to him makes no difference. Younger men like Zemlinsky, Schoenberg, Schreker and, youngest of all, E.W. Korngold show a related Austrian strain. Of course the most recent paths of Schoenberg and his followers head far away from their starting-point. Young people love Mahler and his art, and thus his right to the future cannot be taken from him. Conductors who have modeled themselves on him and revere his memory are active in behalf of his works. Thus he will not be 'lost to the world', and his life will not echo in posterity with the unresolved appoggiatura with which *Das Lied von der Erde,* uncertain of destiny, looks into the future, but with the full triad (in the key of the sublime, see Example 21) turning from minor to major in the closing movement of the Ninth.[92]

Example 21. Ninth Symphony, last movement, mm. 183-5

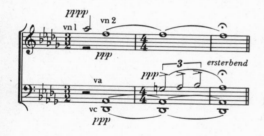

MAHLER AND GUIDO ADLER

by Edward R. Reilly

MAHLER AND GUIDO ADLER

A number of aspects of the relationship between Guido Adler (1855-1941) and Gustav Mahler (1860-1911) have never been entirely clear.[1] Adler insisted that he belonged to Mahler's most intimate circle of friends but was reluctant to discuss the details of their friendship in his published writings. His reticence in this regard, coupled with a variety of other circumstances, has left biographers with scanty and somewhat confusing evidence upon which to form their own opinions.

Adler's brief study of Mahler, first published in 1914, was originally conceived as a memorial essay for a necrological year-book,[2] a type of publication that inevitably restricted the length and scope of the work. In addition, Adler's 'scientific' approach to the study of music history caused him to refrain deliberately from introducing personal matters to 'enhance' his delineation of Mahler's character and work. When the essay was published as a separate volume in 1916, Adler remarked in a newly added foreword that 'Any discussion of my personal relations [with Mahler] was excluded on the ground that my intention was to view the subject from a higher plane.'[3] Adler's references to Mahler in other works clarify a few details but do not add substantially to the basic information provided in the essay. Unquestionably the essay itself was carefully researched, but Adler's failure to indicate sources for some dubious statements or to correct several slips which, although inadvertent, are rather major, has also raised questions about his basic reliability.[4]

Published writings by others on Mahler, and the previously available published letters of the composer, do not clarify the picture of his relations with Adler. Indeed, without some knowledge of the circumstances involved, the appearance of only one of Mahler's letters to Adler in the collection issued in 1924 seems especially puzzling, since in that letter Mahler shows considerable irritation with the historian.

The works of Paul Stefan (who was perhaps closest personally to Adler),[5] Richard Specht and other early writers on Mahler offer

77

little or nothing beyond the information provided by Adler himself. In Alma Mahler's *Gustav Mahler, Erinnerungen und Briefe,* however, the few references to Adler are largely unflattering[6] and might well raise doubts as to the degree of friendship between the composer and the historian. Natalie Bauer-Lechner seems to have been on friendlier terms with Adler, but some of her references to him in her recollections also may be interpreted as disparaging.[7]

Although Adler was generally averse to a detailed biographical approach in his own works, preferring a selective manner that singled out what he considered essential personal and musical traits, he was fully aware of the importance of all types of biographical evidence. As a result, he carefully preserved a considerable number of letters and documents connected with musicians and other well-known figures whom he encountered during his long life. This collection, acquired by the University of Georgia in 1953, contains among other items ten letters of varying length from Mahler to Adler together with fifteen cards and a variety of other material. The entire body of Adler's papers is now housed in the Special Collections division of the University of Georgia Library.

In surveying the Mahler documents in the Adler collection, one's initial reaction may well be a sense of disappointment. The letters do not offer major new insights into Mahler's character or work, nor do they provide answers to the more important questions connected with Mahler's early years. A few present vivid glimpses of Mahler's personality; the larger number, dating from the last fifteen years of the composer's life, are hasty messages written to deal with some immediate practical matter. Yet, upon closer study, especially in connection with the other documents that refer to Mahler in the collection, the letters gain in significance both in the narrower biographical sense and in the broader cultural and historical context.

Examples of a thirty-year friendship between the leading composer and the leading musicologist of a country are far from commonplace. Guido Adler, in many respects the true founder of musicology in Austria, understood his mission as more than editing and interpreting the music of past epochs. Although some new styles may have seemed strange to him, he was open to music of his own time, that is, the music of Richard Wagner and the generation immediately after Wagner. Adler's respect for artistic expression and his capacity for enthusiasm, which he preserved well into old age, required him to encourage the young, the aspiring and the unrecognized, and to make their work accessible to the general public. This role as mentor, which he allotted himself, Adler played not only in relation to Mahler, for whom he had early conceived an almost fatherly affection, but also in relation to other composers who were personally more distant, among them Arnold Schoenberg.

Already in the year 1880 we see Adler attempting to give practical help to his young friend Gustav Mahler. The story of this friendship, which we will attempt to trace in the pages that follow, is essentially a story of recommendations, interventions and projects that the musical scholar designed for the benefit of the composer, which were intended to assure his material well-being and his artistic position. For about thirty years, until Mahler's death, Adler stood up for him with words and deeds, unperturbed if some of the deeds miscarried or if some unsolicited words of advice irritated Mahler. And even after Mahler's death Adler did everything within his power to advance the work of his friend and to honor his memory.

The roots of the friendship between Adler and Mahler lay in the profound idealism that they shared. Both had set their hearts on music in earliest youth, and in an epoch in which music, and art in general, possessed a place of esteem in the consciousness of youth that it is hardly possible to imagine today. The music dramas and writings of Wagner, the plays of Ibsen and the novels of Dostoevsky had produced a cultural climate that led many young men to devote themselves to art and to expect from art a regeneration of the world. Mahler's friend Siegfried Lipiner (1856-1911) fervently hoped for a revival of religion from art[8] and with thoughts of this kind exercised the strongest influence on Mahler. Other artists and writers on politics who worked in Vienna around 1880 strove through the means of art for a renewal of morality, of society and of all of life.[9] These like-minded people, whose views and paths often diverged later on, viewed each other as friends and in their friendship seemed to promote an almost romantic cult. The friendship of Mahler and Adler also stemmed from that era in which the enthusiasm for everything German, for Richard Wagner, for vegetarianism and for social reform, created an amalgam, which survived the years of youth in a purified form.

Earlier writers on Mahler constantly stress idealism and all-embracing love as the core of his work. In more recent research, however, these elements often receive much less attention than the darker, more tragic or ironic, sides of his nature. The roots of the suffering reflected in his compositions are not difficult to find in his family background and childhood experiences. His idealism, on the other hand, seems an unlikely product of such experiences. It seems to stem from the spiritual adventures of his early years in Vienna, about which Mahler research still knows very little. The same time and place were equally important in forming the ideals of Guido Adler.

Before we re-examine the story of the friendship between Mahler and Adler in the light of the material in the Adler collection, a few points concerning the letters must be noted. Among Adler's papers none of his own letters to Mahler is preserved and thus far none has been traced in other collections. Also, very few of Mahler's letters are dated and the envelopes have not been preserved. Thus, except for a few of the cards, postmarks cannot be used to determine when the messages were written. As a result, some of the letters and cards pose difficult problems in dating. For some items only tentative dates can be suggested; the events mentioned in others indicate the time of origin more clearly.

The careers of Mahler and Adler parallel one another in rather general, but important, ways. Both came from Jewish families, spent their early years in Iglau (Jihlava) and attended the Conservatory and University (Mahler informally) in Vienna. Both built early reputations away from Vienna, Mahler as a conductor in a variety of different posts, Adler as a scholar and teacher at the German University in Prague. And both returned to high-ranking positions in Vienna within a year of one another, Mahler in 1897 as conductor and then Artistic Director at the Court Opera, and Adler in 1898 as Hanslick's successor as Professor of Music History at the University of Vienna.

Precisely when Adler met Mahler is uncertain. Both grew up in Iglau and, in a later talk on Mahler, Adler gave the following colorful description of the place:

We enter a little provincial town on the border of Moravia and Bohemia: a nationally isolated German-speaking enclave with an ancient culture, with a mining privilege and a cloth workers' company from the Middle Ages, the different faiths living in peace side by side, with ever-increasing aspirations on the part of the Czech minority in relation to the propertied Germans, who occupy the [administration of the] government and guide it conscientiously. A large, wide square with archaic buildings is in the middle of the town. There in a corner stands the Catholic Church and next to it the barracks, the changing garrisons of which enliven the humdrum society; and the young officers in particular lend color to the picture of the town's main street and put the hearts of the young girls in a whirl. The students – members of the Iglavia student association – also add color during the University holidays with their gay-colored caps.[10]

In his memoirs, *Wollen und Wirken* (1935), Adler further stresses the harmony between the Catholic priests and the Jewish rabbi, J. J. Unger.[11] Thus, although Adler's experiences in this regard may have been different from those of Mahler, it is also possible that Mahler's initial exposure to anti-Semitism may have been somewhat later than is generally supposed. Like Mahler's, Adler's musical training also began in Iglau, and they both studied with the same piano teacher, Brosch, Adler several years before Mahler.[12]

In spite of their common background and 'home town', Mahler and Adler were not childhood friends, as is sometimes stated.[13] Adler himself is a little ambiguous on this point in his specific writings on Mahler but clarifies the matter in his memoirs. Adler, five years older than Mahler, left Iglau in 1864 to continue his education in Vienna. He 'first became acquainted with Gustav Mahler when he [Mahler] came to Vienna as a pupil of the Conservatory'.[14] Thus the time of their meeting can be narrowed to the years 1875-8, but when they encountered each other within this period remains uncertain. Adler himself attended the Conservatory from 1868 to 1874 and certainly remained in touch with some of his teachers (notably Bruckner) and fellow students after that time. He began working on a degree in law at the University of Vienna in 1873 (completed in 1878) and went on to earn a doctorate in music history (completed in 1880) at the same institution, where he then served as an unsalaried lecturer until his move to Prague. Thus he was in Vienna during the entire period that Mahler was a student there. Adler's major teachers at the Conservatory differed somewhat from those of Mahler, but his picture of the strengths and weaknesses of the institution[15] certainly reflects the feelings of many young students active there at about the same time as Mahler.

Common homeland, religious heritage and devotion to music may well have provided the initial basis for friendship between Adler and Mahler. It is possible that the two families had been acquainted, or had common friends, in Iglau, and that Adler helped the newly-arrived Mahler to learn his way around Vienna. But another, equally important and more demonstrable, bond in their early years was their fervent admiration for Wagner and his music. In 1872, when Adler was only seventeen years old, he and his friends Felix Mottl and Karl Wolf (not Hugo Wolf, as some writers indicate) had officially formed the Wiener akademischer Wagner-Verein to promote Wagner's works in the Austrian capital.[16] Later, probably in 1875, these youthful enthusiasts met the composer during one of his visits to Vienna. Subsequently Adler attended performances of the *Ring* at Bayreuth in 1876, of *Parsifal* in 1882 and of *Tristan* in 1886 (the same years as the visits of Bruckner). From the published annual reports of the Wagner-Verein, Mahler is known to have joined in 1877. He left it in 1879, at the same time as his friends Anton Krisper, Rudolf Krzyzanowsky and Hans Rott.[17] Thus, in all probability Adler and Mahler were at least well acquainted during these years.

The first manuscript document among Adler's papers that links him with Mahler comes from another member of the Wagner society, Franz Schaumann, who had been Adler's companion on his visit to Bayreuth in 1876 and was later to become chairman of the society.[18] Schaumann's letter is obviously in reply to a query made by Adler in Mahler's behalf:

No. 81 [Schaumann's identifying number]

Vienna, 10 April 1880

Dear Adler!

In reply to your letter of the 8th of the month, permit me to inform you that although the choirmaster post is not yet definitely filled, an individual is already under consideration for it: Mahler, whose artistic aspiration is well known to me, would, with the exception of the direction of the concerts, hardly find a [suitable] sphere of activity; for in such positions it is less a matter of artistic ability than of a rather mechanical musician's experience.

Just because of the friendly opinion that I cherish for Mahler's talents, I would advise against such a post, simply because of his competence; for he would certainly be disillusioned in the first weeks.

With cordial greetings,

Yours,

F. Schaumann[19]

The particulars of the post mentioned are as yet unknown. What is perhaps most interesting about the letter, however, is that it shows that Mahler's idealism and devotion to artistic goals were already obvious to those who knew him at this age. At the same time it shows Adler already assuming the role that he was to play repeatedly in his relations with Mahler. Recognizing his qualities, Adler from the first worked actively to help him in whatever way he could.

The first currently-known mention of Adler by Mahler is found in a postcard preserved in the *Handschriftensammlung* of the Vienna Stadtbibliothek. In this card, which is directed to Dr Richard Kralik and carries a postmark of January 1883, Mahler requests that the 'Commer volume' (almost certainly referring to Franz Commer (1813-87), editor of several important collections of early music) should be delivered to 'Dr Adler'. Clearly Guido Adler is meant.[20]

The earliest direct communication between Mahler and Adler among the latter's papers seems to be a calling-card. The various references found on it suggest the year 1886. The card, with *Gustav Mahler* printed on its face, bears the following note on the reverse side:

Dear Friend! The Gervinus is enclosed with thanks. I remember that you promised some time ago a recommendation to *Paul* or Fritsch etc. If possible, please send it to me at my present address: *G.M. in Iglau.* Farewell – *see you again soon!*

The Gervinus mentioned is certainly the literary critic and historian Georg Gottfried Gervinus (1805-71), and the accompanying book may have been his well-known *Händel und Shakespeare* (1868). The other two names may be tentatively identified as Oskar Paul (1836-98), a professor of music at the University of Leipzig with whom Adler had already corresponded, and the Leipzig publisher of Wagner's collected prose works, E. W. Fritzsch (*sic*). The location of both men suggests that the card probably dates from the summer of 1886, immediately before Mahler took up the post of second conductor at Leipzig. From Mahler's letters to Friedrich Löhr,[21] we know that Mahler planned to stay in Iglau from 15 to 24 July, before going to Leipzig.

The German text of this brief note shows that Mahler was already using the intimate *Du* form of address. Adler had taken up his appointment as Professor of Music History at the German University in Prague in 1885 at about the same time that Mahler began work at the German Theater there. Thus during this period Mahler and Adler were probably in close touch with one another, and Adler had ample experience of Mahler's work as an opera conductor. In his study Adler also notes that he attended a very-well-received performance of Beethoven's Ninth Symphony.[22] In the draft of an article on the German Theater in Prague written in 1887 or 1888 (a published version has not been traced as yet), Adler already mentions Mahler's distinctive work as a conductor: 'In Herr Gustav Mahler, the present young conductor of the City Theater in Leipzig, the Opera possessed a leader both youthfully fresh and exemplary, who in stormy assault conquered the hearts of the listeners [*crossed out* – if not the critics also].' To this he adds the amusing comment: 'His ardor kindled exaltation but also not infrequently smashed the conductor's lamps.'

Chronologically the next group of documents connected with Mahler among Adler's papers are those associated with Mahler's appointment as Director of the Royal Hungarian Opera in Budapest in 1888. One of the few services in behalf of his friend that Adler acknowledges in his study is his recommendation of Mahler for this post.[23] In response to a query from the distinguished 'cellist David Popper (1843-1913), then in Budapest, Adler strongly endorsed Mahler for the vacant position. Adler's side of the correspondence has not survived, but three letters by Popper dealing with the Budapest position are found among Adler's papers. These letters, fortunately all dated, shed some light on the details of the matter,[24] and suggest just how insistent Adler's backing was. At the time of this exchange with Popper, Adler was at Siegenfeld bei Baden for his summer holiday.

Königswart, 4 July 1888

Esteemed Herr Professor,

In immediate reply to your kind lines, let me inform you that I will convey their principal contents, regarding Herr G. Mahler, to the proper place; there where the decisions about the ultimate filling of the long-pending Pest position, a kind of dragging old sea monster, will finally be made.

Let us hope for the best outcome: I wish for it with you. Fourteen days ago I left the business at the stage in which serious negotiations, which were apparently going well, were in progress with a very renowned foreign conductor. That may have changed over-night since then, as so often in this case. In any event I will inform you of the actual outcome of my step. Until then I am, with sincere regards,

Yours,   D. Popper

Königswart, 11 July 1888

Most esteemed Herr Professor,

Enclosed [is] the answer of Director von Mihalovich[25] to my letter in the Mahler affair. Naturally it will not end there, and as is expressly stated in the letter, Herr Mahler will be the object of the most searching inquiry very soon, if by chance Mottl's[26] engagement is not settled in the meantime.

I have declared myself strongly for Mahler, but as you can perceive from the enclosed letter, the opera and concert conductor, obviously presumed highly gifted, is considered only secondarily: first of all the gentlemen have their focus on the organizational ability and activity of the future opera director, to whom will fall the thorough cleansing of an artistic Augean stable.

Now patience is called for! The decision cannot be kept waiting for long: when in autumn the first leaves fall, then many scales will fall from the eyes of the by-no-means-to-be-envied new Pest opera director! For the rest, the position is splendidly endowed (10000 fl.), and that is, after all, a kind of consolation!

With the request for the due return of the Mihalovich letter and with kindest greetings, I am always most willingly,

Your faithfully devoted,   D. Popper

Königswart, 17 July 1888

Most esteemed Herr Professor,

Certainly the personal acquaintance of *Kapellmeister* Mahler would please and interest me highly, but to what purpose would we burden the interesting but very busy man with the hardships of a journey here! I am at best only a go-between – never a principal in the pending matter, and my interest in it is solely artistic, almost excluding everything personal. On the other hand, a reciprocal personal exchange between Herren von Mihalovich and Mahler on the hallowed ground in Bayreuth would appear to me thoroughly appropriate and advantageous.

I was indeed very pleased by your complete backing of Mahler the 'human being.' This important passage in your letter will be of weighty significance for the complete evaluation of the possible Budapest directorial candidate, and since you yourself have authorized me to do so, I am sending your last letter in its entirety to Herr von Mihalovich.

With best wishes for your summer stay, I am most respectfully,

Yours,   D. Popper

These letters indicate both the uncertainty of the situation with regard to the position in Budapest and the active and vital support that Adler gave to Mahler. In spite of Popper's remarks in the third of these letters, he took the time toward the middle of August to hear Mahler conduct his version of Weber's *Die drei Pintos* in Prague. Favorably impressed, Popper had discussions with Mahler and then recommended him for the post in Budapest. In September Mahler met in Vienna with a representative of the *Intendant* of the Budapest opera company, Franz von Beniczky, and almost immediately went to the Hungarian capital, where his contract was settled on the 28th.[27]

The second of the presently-known communications from Mahler to Adler may well date from this same time. Since Adler's wife is referred to in it, it could not belong to the period before 1887. The contents of the letter suggest a connection with Adler's proposal that Mahler should meet Mihalovich in Bayreuth, a meeting that was apparently made unnecessary by Popper's visit to Prague. The letter is marked as written in Prague, where in the summer of 1888 Angelo Neumann had engaged Mahler to conduct *Die drei Pintos* and *Der Barbier von Bagdad*.[28] A quarrel between Mahler and Neumann led to Mahler's dismissal before the latter work was actually performed. At the same time Mahler was at work drafting the first movement of his Second Symphony.

Dear Friend!

Just quickly my sincerest thanks and acknowledgment of the receipt of your letter. The business about Bayreuth and Königswart I must first think over a little more - here I have my hands full now - and at present do not know how I can get away. - I am now really curious about how all that will turn out. As soon as something further happens, I will let you know.

Please give my best regards to your wife; I am, with most cordial greetings,

Your very hurried

Prague. Saturday.   Mahler

The years from 1889 to 1897 are at present a total blank with regard to concrete evidence of contacts between Mahler and Adler. Adler's papers contain no letters or other documents associated with Mahler during this period, and thus raise the question of whether other letters of Mahler to Adler may have been lost, destroyed or given away.[29] Certainly later events and letters imply no break in their friendship. In all probability actual meetings between the two were rather less frequent during this time because of their different locations; but there may well have been visits in Prague, Vienna or Steinbach.

During this period Adler was extremely active in a variety of areas. From 1884 to 1894 he was one of the editors of the *Vierteljahrsschrift für Musikwissenschaft*, which he had founded with Philipp Spitta (1841-94) and Friedrich Chrysander (1826-1901). In the late 1880s he began to plan the well-known historical series that ultimately appeared under the name Denkmäler der Tonkunst in Österreich. As trial volumes his editions of the musical works by the Habsburg emperors Ferdinand III, Leopold I and Joseph I were issued in 1892 and 1893. He also headed the music division of the great music and theater exposition of 1892 in Vienna and prepared its impressive catalogue.[30] These and other activities brought him into contact with many important figures in the Austrian aristocracy and governmental bureaucracy whose support he needed for his undertakings. In the musical sphere, in spite of his enthusiasm for Wagner, he had already gained the backing of Hanslick in 1880 with his first major historical study, 'Die historischen Grundklassen der christlich-abendländischen Musik bis 1600'.[31] Perhaps through Hanslick he won Brahms' support for the Denkmäler. All of these various undertakings kept Adler in close touch with the musical world of Vienna (as well as other European centers), in spite of his residence in Prague, and put him in a position to aid Mahler's candidacy for a conducting post at the Vienna Court Opera in 1897. In his study he notes that he again backed his friend when the *Intendant*, Baron Bezecny, 'turned to me with regard to his doubts'.[32] No written confirmation of this recommendation is found in Adler's papers, but there is no reason to question his statement. In this case he probably discussed Mahler's abilities directly with Bezecny, who became a member of the Board of Directors of the Denkmäler this same year (1897).

Documents connecting Mahler and Adler resume in 1897 with an undated note from Mahler to his close friend and lawyer Emil Freund. Mahler indicates that 'Adler writes just now that if my *curriculum vitae* is not in his hands within two days the whole business must be left standing until autumn. Thus send it off immediately.'[33] The 'business' referred to is certainly, as indicated in a note in the *Briefe,* Adler's plan to secure a grant from the Gesellschaft zur Förderung deutscher Wissenschaft, Kunst und Literatur in Böhmen for the publication of Mahler's First and Third Symphonies and the orchestral parts for the Second. The entire affair assumes prior contact and consultation between Mahler and Adler, for which no documents have been traced.

A passage in Natalie Bauer-Lechner's *Erinnerungen* indicates that by New Year's Day of 1898 Mahler was already sure that he would receive the subsidy,[34] and a letter of 21 January to his Hamburg friend Hermann Behn confirms a break with Hofmeister, the publisher of the score of the Second Symphony and Behn's piano reduction.[35] Official action by the society seems to have been taken only after some kind of informal decision had been reached, for the two reports that Adler submitted to the Gesellschaft, copies of which are found among his papers, are dated 23 and 24 January 1898. It is also possible, however, that the original recommendations had been made earlier, and that the existing manuscripts were copies designed for some other project.

The first of these reports, consisting of two legal-size pages, is probably based directly on the *curriculum vitae* mentioned by Mahler. It contains a summary review of Mahler's life and activity, especially his professional activity as a conductor and composer, with references to performances and publications of his works through the Third Symphony. This material was later incorporated to some extent in Adler's study and offers little that is new to modern students. It is perhaps interesting to note that, in reviewing Mahler's output, reference is still made to the early operas, songs and chamber music: 'In his youth (up to 1880) he composed chamber-music pieces, songs and an opera *Die Argonauten;* from 1880-1890 a fairy-tale opera *Rübezahl,* for which, like the aforementioned, he also wrote the text; in addition *Lieder eines fahrenden Gesellen...* and after some symphonic essays, the First Symphony in D major...' *Das klagende Lied* is mentioned separately. Also the group of five *Wunderhorn* songs including 'Der schildwache Nachtlied', 'Verlor'ne Müh!', 'Wir geniessen die himmlischen Freuden', 'Trost im Unglück' and 'Wer hat dies Liedlein erdacht' are still listed under their original name, *Humoresken,* first as orchestral songs and later as songs with piano accompaniment *already published* by Hofmeister in Leipzig. Since no such edition by Hofmeister of these songs is known, the possibility that there were concrete plans for this firm to issue them deserves further investigation.

This first report was apparently used again for some later purpose as yet unknown (perhaps to approach another publisher?), for Adler subsequently added several lines indicating that the First and Second Symphonies[36] were then appearing with the support of the Gesellschaft. Warm support is also contained in the appended postscript: 'I personally value Mahler uncommonly – as a human being (as an intimate friend) and as an artist. He always has the artistic ideal in view.'

The longer, four-page *Referat* is devoted specifically to Mahler's first three symphonies. It opens with a discussion of the historical position of the symphonies in relation to the then-modern tendency toward expansion in time and musical means, already equating Mahler in this regard with Richard Strauss: 'In this respect Mahler and Richard Strauss stand in the same line, and, to speak frankly, also at the head of the most modern movement in music.' The actual discussion of the symphonies is similar in nature to that found in Adler's later essay, with special emphasis on their purely musical structure, in spite of their poetic titles, and on literary and philosophical themes as stimuli to purely musical utterance. Some of the characteristic features of the individual symphonies are outlined, in general in an enthusiastic manner but not without a few reservations, such as a reference to the 'unprecedented cacophonies' of the third movement of the Third Symphony. (A single page of notes on the Third Symphony, on the official stationery of the Vienna Court Opera, suggests that Adler had discussed the work directly with Mahler shortly before he wrote his report.) In a passage concerning the Second Symphony, Adler shows how radical the work seemed in terms of contemporary aesthetics, and implies that Mahler's works might eventually lead to new concepts of the nature of music.

In the Second Symphony (C minor) the bold power of combination builds up to harmonies previously not to be found in the literature. *In this respect he oversteps the boundary previously accepted in our time for the purely beautiful* [italics mine]. It is not impossible, and not improbable – indeed surmise based on the experience of history suggests – that the progressive artist leads his own age and especially posterity to another way of viewing and understanding sounds. Whether an enduring advance results...only the future can decide.

In a letter to Adler written several years later (see below, p. 97), Mahler takes a playful dig at another aspect of this view of him violating the canons of beauty. Referring to his future wife, Alma Schindler, he writes jokingly: 'If you know her, you know everything; if not, I must again overstep the boundaries of art and attempt to paint with words.' Although Mahler perhaps deliberately misconstrued Adler's point in this case, the passing reference nevertheless suggests that the limits of music had been a frequent topic of conversation between them, and one which bore fruit in Mahler's changing views about the use of voices in his symphonic works. As all students of Mahler's works know, the three symphonies written after the Fourth are entirely instrumental, and in the later works voices appear in all movements or in none.

Adler concludes his report by indicating that the large forces required for the performance of the works considered, which permit their presentation 'only at larger places with large orchestras, or at music festivals', make it difficult to find a publisher for them. An estimate of the cost of printing by Eberle and Co. in Vienna for the scores, keyboard reductions and parts for the First and Third Symphonies, and for the parts of the Second, is given as 12 000 gulden.[37] On Adler's recommendation, Eberle is reported willing to undertake the publication if a partial grant for the printing costs can be obtained. The specific recommendation is for 3000 florins,[38] payable in two installments, one immediately, the other in January 1899. When the works were actually published, the Josef Weinberger company acted as selling agent for Eberle.

Adler's success in obtaining this grant for the printing of Mahler's symphonies is now widely known, although his study makes no mention of the fact that the plan was his own.[39] The importance of the publication of these compositions can hardly be overestimated, for it is from this time that Mahler began to gain widespread recognition as a symphonic composer. As he had done in Mahler's career as a conductor, Adler came forward with concrete assistance at a critical point in Mahler's development as a composer. That Adler already viewed Mahler with Richard Strauss as at the forefront of symphonic composers shows an evaluation of Mahler's creations that was as yet shared by only a few contemporaries.

Mahler's letters to Adler resume in 1898. A brief note may be dated shortly before the performance of Mahler's First Symphony that took place in Prague on 3 March 1898.

Dear Friend!

Agreed! We will save my 'private production' for better times. Thus we will see each other at my orchestral rehearsal. I am putting up at the Hotel *Stern*.

Most cordially your old
Gustav Mahler

This time, dear friend, please do not count on me for your entertainments. I must save all my time for myself – for revisions – corrections, etc. etc.[40]

This note obviously points to other visits to Adler during the preceding period. Adler is already among those friends for whom Mahler goes through his work in private, and who, when possible, attend Mahler's rehearsals. In connection with this performance of the First Symphony, without the 'Blumine' movement that Mahler discarded in his final version of the work, a draft of a brief review, probably intended for one of the local newspapers, is found among Adler's papers. In it he describes the enthusiastic reception given the work. The performance was directed by Mahler but had been prepared by Franz Schalk (1863-1931), at that time an opera conductor in Prague.

Another letter, which cannot as yet be dated with certainty, may well belong to this same period and indicate the nature of the 'private production' referred to in the note given above. Plans for what appears to be an informal run-through of the Second Symphony are discussed. The 'Walker' mentioned is the American singer Edyth Walker (1867-1950), who was active at the Vienna Court Opera from 1895 to 1903. In his reference to a Verein, Mahler perhaps means the Gesellschaft sponsoring the publication of his symphonies.

Dear Friend!

I am simply *stunned*! I will definitely come with a pianist to play you my 2nd; naturally the alto solo is really best sung. Perhaps I will bring *Walker* to do it. She could possibly perform many other things of mine. – I do this as a kind of thanks for the Verein, and will make certain to set a day for it convenient for you. We will correspond further about it. If this cannot be combined with the concert, I will make an extra trip!

Most cordially, in haste, your grateful
Gustav Mahler

In the fall of 1898 Adler took up his new post at the University of Vienna. He gave his public inaugural lecture, entitled 'Musik und Musikwissenschaft' (Music and Musicology), at the University on 26 October. The *Neue musikalische Presse* (30 October) reports that many notable figures of the day attended, including Mahler and Siegfried Lipiner. Unfortunately, we have no record of their reactions to Adler's presentation, in which he stressed the importance of the connections between scholarship and living art (the concluding lines of this lecture appear at the beginning of this volume). The following letter, however, shows that Mahler had already been in touch with Adler by late August or early September.

Warmest thanks, dear Friend!

Forgive me for not having looked you up yet, but I am harried to death and do not have a minute for myself. - It will interest you that I am performing *Donna Diana* by Reznicek.[41] Because of its freshness the work is uncommonly attractive to me and I believe that it will have a great success. I hope to see you soon. Would you be interested in seeing the *Götterdämmerung* newly rehearsed by me with an (excellent) new cast? *Sunday, September 4!* If you would like to come, let me know in time. Most cordially, with many greetings to your wife,

Your,

Gustav Mahler

From this time onward the number of Mahler's communications with Adler increases and, except for the briefest notes, most of the letters can be dated with greater certainty. The fact that both men were living in Vienna, however, naturally limits the character of their correspondence. Most of the more interesting letters were written when Mahler was away from the city, especially during the summers, and the bulk of the remainder deal with immediate social or professional matters. A card postmarked 12 November 1898 is characteristic of more than half a dozen short messages. In a number of these, however, the subject is by no means as clear as in the present case:

Dear Friend! Do you own a score of the *Fantastique* of Berlioz? And can you lend it to me for a few days? If necessary, *where* can one get hold of it *quickly*?

Most cordially your G. Mahler

Write to me at the Opera, please![42]

It was also during the year 1898 that Mahler, through Adler's efforts, became a member of the Board of Directors of the Denkmäler der Tonkunst in Österreich, filling the vacancy created by the death of Brahms in the preceding year. Adler's recommendation of Mahler for the position, dated 23 October 1898, is preserved in the Alte Verwaltungsarchiv (old administrative archive) of the Denkmäler Gesellschaft, and shows several parallels with the two *Referate* discussed earlier.[43] How seriously Mahler took the position is uncertain. Adler says only that he was an 'effective member'[44] of the board. Henry-Louis de La Grange reports that, in an unpublished passage, Natalie Bauer-Lechner's diary (New Year's Day, 1900) records Mahler telling her and Josef Stritzko of the publishing firm Waldheim-Eberle of his exasperation at the time wasted at one of the meetings of the Denkmäler board. How little Mahler actually knew of the series at that time is indicated by the reported comment that it contained only works of poor quality from the preceding century.[45] Of the thirteen volumes published up to 1900 only three had contained works of the eighteenth century. And few musicians today would agree that the compositions actually included by men such as Heinrich Isaac (*c.* 1450-1517), Johann Jakob Froberger (1616-67), Johann Joseph Fux (1660-1741) and others are of poor quality. Rather Mahler's comments suggest the limitations of his own perspective at the time. The available evidence does not indicate whether this perspective may have changed in the years that followed. Nor do we know to what extent he may have given Adler assistance in the form of verbal reactions to some of the various works planned for publication in the series. His actual attendance at the meetings of the board seems to have been sporadic (see the two notes quoted below, pp. 98 and 99).[46] That he actually possessed copies of both the Austrian and German Denkmäler series is confirmed by letters of Alma Mahler in which she asks Adler to dispose of them after her husband's death.

The year 1899 is generally bare of documents. It can be safely assumed, however, that Adler and Mahler remained in close touch with one another and that Adler heard many of Mahler's performances at the Vienna Opera. Clippings of a number of newspaper reviews of operas conducted by Mahler are found among Adler's papers. A note from Justine Mahler (later Rosé), probably dating from this year, is an invitation to a social evening, which may well have been one of many similar gatherings.

In her diary for 17 April 1900 Natalie Bauer-Lechner notes
Mahler's critical reaction to Adler's views of two matters,
Wagner's use of the chorus and Mozart's supposed ability to write
out the parts for the Overture to *Don Giovanni* without first
having at least sketched a score.[47] As reported, it is difficult to
determine what Adler actually said. With regard to Wagner, he
seems to have commented negatively on some unidentified aspects
of Wagner's writings and on the diminished role of the chorus in
his mature works. Mahler apparently brooked no criticism of any
kind with respect to Wagner, regardless of the fact that he knew of
Adler's own admiration of the composer. The Mozart discussion
seems to have centered around the oft-repeated story of how
Mozart wrote out the Overture to *Don Giovanni* at the last
minute. Mahler, as an experienced composer, had quite solid
grounds for doubting any composer's ability to write out a full set
of parts for a score that he had not at least sketched on paper. In
her diary for the following spring (18 April 1901), Bauer-Lechner
reports yet another difference of opinion between the two friends.
The subject in this case had to do with the merits of Tchaikovsky's
Sixth Symphony, with Adler defending the work and Mahler
sharply attacking it.[48] These differences, cited separately (as they
have been in the past), may suggest that Mahler was more critical
of Adler than actually seems to have been the case. Mahler was
never known for his politeness in discussion, and the terms in
which he expressed disagreement often bordered on the insulting.
But both Mahler and Adler were noted for their directness, and
the incidents just noted indicate clearly the freedom with which
they could openly disagree. Adler, unlike many of Mahler's
admirers, never seems to have been over-awed by him.

In June 1900, Mahler took the Vienna Philharmonic Orchestra
to Paris for a series of concerts at the International Exposition.
Two letters in Adler's files show that he made inquiries for Mahler
about arrangements for the orchestra in the French capital. One,
from a certain François Benkey to an unidentified 'Herr Baron',[49]
suggests that Adler in turn had asked one of his connections to
seek further information about a suitable agent. Benkey reports
that R. Strakosch had been recommended to him in this connection. The other letter, dated 2 February, is from Romain Rolland
(1866-1944), with whom Adler was then in touch concerning the
musicological sessions of the meeting of the International Society

for Comparative History in Paris. Rolland provides much more
specific information about the various alternatives available.
'Official' attendance at the Exposition could be arranged through
the head of the music committee, in which case the orchestra
would perform in the acoustically bad 'grande salle du Tro-
cadéro'. 'Unofficial' attendance would require an agent and a
hall; Rolland recommends M. Demets and the Nouveau Théâtre
on the rue Blanche, where the Thursday concerts of the Colonne
Orchestra took place. Rolland continues: 'These concerts of the
Viennese orchestra would doubtless be of great interest to us,
especially in a period in which there is a true curiosity in Paris
about German conductors.' Rolland's warning about the Tro-
cadéro auditorium seems not to have been fully heeded, since the
last two of the three Philharmonic concerts were given there.[50]
The financial, if not the critical, failure of the Paris concerts is
common knowledge, and Adler notes in his essay that Mahler had
to obtain the money to pay for the deficit from a 'Viennese artistic
Maecenas'.[51] Whether Adler was in Paris at the time of the concerts is uncertain; it seems unlikely, since in the following month
he was obligated to attend the historical congress mentioned
above.

A short note from Mahler later this summer indicates tentative
plans for a possible meeting with Adler, which apparently did not
take place.

Maiernigg, 2 August [1900]

Dear Friend!

It is hardly possible for me to settle on a definite meeting, for just now I
am busy here with the completion of my 4th, and in addition must be
ready to set off for Vienna. Yet it is not impossible that I will take a little
bicycle excursion in the Dolomites in the next few [days], and in this event
will try to reach you in the Pension Saxonia in Innichen. Most cordially in
great haste

Your Mahler

Please give *Hofrat* Hanslick my regards, should you have the opportunity.

On 10 August Mahler did actually go off on his bicycle in what
he thought was the direction of Velden, but twice lost his way and
nearly came to grief on one of the mountain slopes.[52]

Later this same year Adler went to Munich to hear Mahler conduct his Second Symphony (on 20 October) with the Kaim
Orchestra. The program of the concert and two articles from

Munich newspapers are found among Adler's papers. After the concert Adler joined Mahler, Natalie Bauer-Lechner and other friends at the Park Hotel. Mahler expatiated on the misunderstandings created by programs connected with his music and attempted to clarify the views that he had expressed in his well-known letter to Arthur Seidl, which had just been published.[53] Adler commented on the varying reactions of Richard Strauss, Karl Muck and Wilhelm Kienzl to earlier performances of the symphony, and especially their attitudes to the use of dissonance in one part of the first movement.[54]

Two of the more interesting letters from Mahler to Adler date from 1901. The first was written during the period of Mahler's recovery at Abbazia (Opatija in modern Yugoslavia) from a hemorrhage that had forced him to take sick leave. The letter shows Mahler's philosophic reaction to his illness, his sense of relief at being freed from his duties as conductor at the Opera and his determination to turn over more responsibility to subordinates.

[*c*. 28 March 1901, from Abbazia]

Dear Friend!

Many thanks for your kind lines. I have been here eight days now and can say that my condition improves from hour to hour. – Easter Sunday [7 April 1901] I will arrive in Vienna healthier than ever. Only now is it apparent that all my sufferings proceed from this cause, which was hidden from the doctors as well as myself. And without this unexpected episode, no one would ever have thought of looking for the source of my suffering where it was found during the general anesthetic.

Thus once more it happens that an apparent misfortune turns out to be the greatest blessing for the person concerned. – Here I live a little in the atmosphere of my 4th, which I am readying for publication, and to which I will put the finishing touches tomorrow or the day after. – As to Vienna, the past weeks have been quite instructive for me, and I hope never again to sink into the whirlpool of this really inferior activity.

From now on I will [be] at the *helm* and leave the oars entirely to the others. But I must still find, or train, some better sailors.

My sister and I greet you cordially and hope that you will return from Karlsbad strengthened, as I can certainly promise of myself.

With friendliest regards,

Gustav Mahler

At the end of the year Adler received a charming letter from Mahler announcing his engagement to Alma Schindler.

[between 22 and 27 December 1901]

My dear Friend!

I have so much for which to thank you – finally also for the superb bust.[55] For a long time my sister and I had intended to visit you out there! But something always intervened. Among other matters, something which you will certainly allow as a valid excuse for me: I have become engaged! It is still a secret and I am telling only my closest friends. My fiancée is Alma Schindler. If you know her, you know everything; if not, I must again overstep the boundaries of art and attempt to paint with words.

[A line cancelled here.]

Forgive me for knowing nothing else to say today, and also preserve your friendship, so valuable to me, into my 'new life'. See you again soon, my dear friend, and most cordial greetings to your dear wife.

Your Mahler

Adler's reaction to this announcement is unknown. A program and program book among his papers indicate that he probably attended the first Vienna performance of the Fourth Symphony, conducted by Mahler on 12 January 1902, just after the news of Mahler's engagement to the twenty-two-year-old Fräulein Schindler had become public. In her *Erinnerungen* Alma Mahler mentions this performance, or one that followed it shortly thereafter on the 20th of the month, and the unpleasantness caused at it when Mahler's friends tried to disrupt the relationship of the engaged couple by telling untruthful stories of her conduct.[56] In recounting this episode, and also in describing an earlier meeting with Mahler's close friend Siegfried Lipiner,[57] Frau Mahler makes no pretense about her intense dislike of most of Mahler's older friends. To what extent her feelings about Adler were the same as those about Lipiner and the other older people within Mahler's circle is uncertain. Adler is not singled out in Frau Mahler's memories of this specific time, and there is little indication of any sharp friction between them in the first years of her marriage to Mahler. Among Adler's papers are twelve letters and cards from Alma Mahler from the period in which Mahler was alive (nine more date from after his death). Most of these are again undated, and thus are not always easily assigned to a specific period; but if the underlying elements of the antagonism that appeared a few years later already existed, they do not appear in the brief notes to Adler that can be assigned to the early years of their acquaintance.

A card that can be dated a week after the first Vienna performance of the Fourth, that is, 19 January 1902, shows that
Mahler slept through a planned meeting of some kind, probably
of the board of the Denkmäler. In excusing himself, he playfully
pokes fun at Adler's academic world:

Dear Friend!
  Yesterday a comic mishap befell me! I had an exhausting 'Feuersnot'
rehearsal until 2 o'clock. Came home, ate and lay down for a quarter of
an hour - fell deeply asleep, and woke up - at 5:30. (Never happened
before.) - I hope this appears a 'valid' excuse, and that I receive your
testimonial on my index. Tomorrow after the 'Klagende Lied' we will be
in the special room at *Leidinger's* (Ring). Will we see each other there?
                          Most cordially your most hurried Mahler

A note from Mahler's sister Justine, who married the violinist
Arnold Rosé the day after Mahler married Alma Schindler in
March of this year, dates from June 1902. In it she mentions the
success of the Third Symphony at Krefeld, noting that it had
'made an enormous sensation, especially among the musicians. G.
will have told you yesterday.'
  From the summer holiday of this year, a postcard with a picture
of the 'Villa Mahler am Wörther See', postmarked 25 August and
dated the 23rd of the month, carries the simple message 'V!
Herzlichst M' in Mahler's hand, with the additional note, 'You
know what this happy message, which accompanies a greeting,
means', from Mahler's friend, the lawyer Emil Freund. Unquestionably the 'message' was that the Fifth Symphony was
completed.
  With the end of the summer, and Mahler's return to Vienna,
the need for written communication once more ceased. None of
the notes and cards connected with Mahler among Adler's papers
can be assigned unequivocally to the remaining months of 1902,
or to the entire following year, although it seems probable that
one or two of the very brief notes from Mahler[58] and his wife
belong to this period.
  Mahler's first daughter, Maria Anna, was born on 3 November
1902. In her reminiscences, Alma Mahler mentions that Adler
was the innocent victim of Mahler's tension shortly before her
delivery. Asking Mahler how Alma was, he received the reply:
'Idiot, I forbid you to ask.'[59] A thank-you note from Frau Mahler
for a gift from Adler is probably connected with the birth of this

child. Another letter of Justine Rosé may possibly date from the summer of 1903. In it she mentions a visit of her brother and the fact that many performances of his works were planned for the following winter.

An unpublished letter of Arnold Schoenberg, dated 16 November 1903,[60] in which the composer introduces himself to Adler, marks the beginning of another acquaintanceship, which was soon to bear on Adler's connections with Mahler.

Contacts between Mahler and Adler are more easily established in 1904. Several letters belong to this time, as well as evidence of other kinds. In January Mahler's new version of Weber's *Euryanthe* was first performed at the Opera, and not long afterward Adler drew attention to this version of the work with an article '"Euryanthe" in neuer Einrichtung' in an issue of the *Zeitschrift der Internationalen Musikgesellschaft*.[61] Maintaining an apparently 'objective' tone, Adler reviews the changes undertaken by Mahler and, while indicating that they do not entirely solve the basic problems of the work, supports its revival.

A note from Mahler to Adler belongs to the first months of this year. As with so many of his letters, it again suggests the exhausting round of activities in which Mahler lived. What Adler had asked of Mahler in this instance is unknown, but it was probably something connected with a meeting of the board of the Denkmäler that took place on January 25.[62]

Dear Friend!
I am sorry (I would have been glad to oblige *you*) – but I am *completely spent* from today's orchestra rehearsal of *Corregidor* (from 10 – 1:30) – after yesterday's *Euryanthe;* and in the evening have an ensemble rehearsal of the same opera. I absolutely must rest for a few hours!
Thus no offence, dear friend. I am also writing to his Excellency Bezecny.

Most cordially your

Mahler

Adler's relations with Arnold Schoenberg (1874-1951) appear to have developed rapidly in 1904. In a letter of 17 February Schoenberg invites Adler to attend a performance of *Verklärte Nacht* 'even though this work at best says what I aspired to four or five years ago, and I have long since gone beyond it...' Late in March Adler was already demonstrating active support for the younger composers in Vienna with a feuilleton in the *Neue freie*

Presse.[63] In this article Adler publicized, again within his own scholarly framework, the activities of the new Vereinigung schaffender Tonkünstler Wiens, in which Alexander von Zemlinsky (1872-1942), Schoenberg, Karl Weigl (1881-1949), Josef von Wöss (1863-1943) and others were active. In addition to his own support, Adler also reports Mahler's willingness to conduct one of the three orchestral concerts planned by the group.

The remaining letters from Schoenberg to Adler from 1904 and early 1905 show that he turned to Adler for help with a number of matters connected with the Vereinigung, and that Adler did all that was within his power for the group. Mahler is mentioned on several occasions. In a letter of 1 June 1904 Schoenberg indicates that, even though the fee is very high, he has reached agreement with the members of the Philharmonic for the planned concerts. He continues: 'The next matter is to induce Herr Director Mahler to meet half-way, above all concerning the arrangement of the rehearsals. I hope that will not be too difficult, and a word from you [could] be of great importance in this regard.'[64] Later this year Schoenberg, in a note of 11 November, thanks Adler for his 'kind intercession', apparently in approaching the Rothschilds for financial support for the hard-pressed Vereinigung. He goes on to say that 'Since we are to see each other today at Mahler's, I hope to find the opportunity for more of it' (i.e. intercession).

Early in the following year another letter of Schoenberg (7 January 1905) reports on progress in approaching one of the Rothschilds. On visiting the home of one of the family (which one is not clear)

... the chief clerk recommended that we use the intercession of Mahler, since otherwise he could offer us little cause for hope. We told this to Mahler and he has now recently declared himself willing to approach R. shortly. That is all that I know about it. Thus the business is up to Mahler.

Thereafter the correspondence between Schoenberg and Adler breaks off for several years and is resumed again only in 1910.

In the meantime, in the course of 1904 Adler was actively preparing another project that potentially involved Mahler, Zemlinsky and Schoenberg, among others, a project that was to have a considerable effect on Adler's interpretation of Mahler's last years. At the request of the Minister of Culture and Education, Wilhelm Ritter von Hartel (d. 1907), Adler drafted a memorandum on a possible governmental take-over and reorganization of the Conservatory of the Gesellschaft der Musikfreunde. In his Mahler study he summarized the situation in 1904, explained the role Mahler was to play as director if the proposal was put into effect and indicated Mahler's willingness to accept the position. Apparently because of changes in ministers, the proposal was not immediately acted upon.[65]

In this account Adler makes no mention of the fact that he himself prepared the memorandum, a point that he clarifies in *Wollen und Wirken,* where he reviews the matter in greater detail.[66] The final form of the memorandum, which also includes suggestions for the possible employment of Zemlinsky and Schoenberg in the reorganized Conservatory, is dated Christmas 1904. A letter of Mahler, apparently written somewhat before the birth of his second daughter (15 June 1904), probably refers to a draft of Adler's report and suggests Mahler's active interest in it.

Dear Friend!
As long as my wife is still up I would like to devote myself to her. As soon as she is confined, I will let you know. Meanwhile I am reading your proposals. We can then in due time discuss everything in detail. I am making notes on specific points only if a particular occurs to me that might possibly require alteration. On the whole, however, a divergence of view can only be discussed verbally.

Thus, see you again soon, and most cordial greetings. As to my wife there is still nothing to report.   M.

A letter from Alma Mahler written during the summer of this year also seems to refer to further discussions of the proposal:

Dear Friend
Most esteemed Professor
I have not written you for so long because I was for the most part so tired and exhausted that I was incapable of anything. I have spoken with G. Nevertheless we have arrived at no answer. – He is in the midst of work and it is impossible for him to get all that clear *now.* – In this I also believe a month makes no difference. At the end of August you can then discuss everything with him. He is not disinclined to the whole yet may propose some alterations. But – all that – viewed from a distance. G. is very industrious. Between ourselves – he is at the end of his 6th. I scarcely see him.
As I said, I am – only fair...

A card from Mahler himself later this summer confirms the completion of the Sixth Symphony and reports the impending return of the family to Vienna. Also mentioned is Adler's major new 'opus', his book on Wagner (*Richard Wagner. Vorlesungen gehalten an der Universität Wien* (Leipzig, Breitkopf and Härtel, 1904)):

Dear Friend!

My 6th is now finished, and I am slowly getting ready to return with bag and baggage to Vienna. How dismal! Yet I hope to see you before long and to get from you the fair copy of your opus, which will also be completed now, and which I will now place with delight before me as a whole. – Send it to my home address, for I find more leisure there; and let me hear something from you besides.

With most cordial greetings to you and your wife, also from Alma, who is still very much occupied with her new opus [their new child, born in June].

Your M.

Mahler's invitation for Adler to send him his work provides the background for an already-published letter of Mahler to his wife (14 October 1904)[67] in which, at the beginning of rehearsals for his Fifth Symphony in Cologne, he indulges in some humorous variations on the line 'How blessed, how blessed to be a shoemaker!', ironically listing some of those for whom success and security were less difficult matters. The refrain, which is also found in other letters of Mahler to his wife, is already a variant of one found in Lortzing's *Zar und Zimmermann:* 'How blessed, how blessed to be still a child!' The list of those blessed includes Richard Strauss ('Oh that I were "quite the mama, quite the papa"', referring to the *Sinfonia domestica*) and ends with Adler ('Oh that I were a Professor of Music and could give lectures on Wagner and have them published'). The references suggest some of the envy that the hard-pressed creative musician must occasionally feel when he compares his lot with that of the composer for whom success has come more easily, or with the more secure position of the musician in academic life. Viewed in the light of Mahler's humorous mocking of academic clichés in his notes to Adler himself, this reference cannot be taken too seriously; but it does again suggest Mahler's well-known distrust of writing about music as compared with direct experience of it.

As to Mahler's attitude toward the possible position at the Conservatory, no further information is found for this time among Adler's papers. There is, however, every reason to believe the truth of Adler's statement that Mahler had agreed to assume the position, should the proposed reorganization go through. Adler would hardly have circulated his proposal without Mahler's concurrence, and Adler's reaction to the later events of Mahler's life is understandable only in the light of his absolute confidence that Mahler could and would assume this post after his resignation from the Opera.

Clippings of newspaper reviews suggest that Adler heard performances of Mahler's Third Symphony in Heidelberg and Vienna in 1904, and the Fifth Symphony in Munich. A published letter of Mahler to his wife confirms that Adler attended a performance of the Fourth Symphony in Graz in 1905: '...after the concert I went off along with Mama and Walter and Adler to the hotel, where we sat very happily with the Mauthners and Kolo Moser and let the Festival assembly go its way in the Schlossberg'.[68] Adler also seems to have heard the Fifth Symphony in Vienna.

Only one card (unexpectedly dated) from Mahler to Adler survives from 1905, again from the summer months. Once more good-humoredly mocking the trappings of scholarship, Mahler announces the completion of the Seventh Symphony – in Latin!

15 August 1905

Lieber Freund!

Septima mea finita est. Credo hoc opus fauste natum et bene gestum. Salutationes plurimas tibi et tuis etiam meae uxoris.

G.M.[69]

Adler's fiftieth birthday, 1 November 1905, marked an occasion on which, more concretely than on any other, Mahler gave direct expression of his reciprocal feeling for his friend. 'With embrace, kiss and the dedication "To my dear friend Guido Adler (who will never be lost to me) as a memento of his fiftieth birthday"', he presented Adler with the autograph score of one of his greatest songs, 'Ich bin der Welt abhanden gekommen'.[70] That Adler carefully refrained from mentioning this gift in any of his published writings on Mahler may give some indication of his feelings about publicizing personal relations in his historical work. He refers to it only in an unpublished *Nachwort*, originally written to conclude his study of 1914 when it was issued in book form in 1916, but he subsequently discarded this afterword in favor of the briefer and less personal *Vorwort* found in the published volume. As will be seen below, this unused document provides important evidence about Adler's reactions to the later events in Mahler's life.

The two critical years, 1906 and especially 1907, are not represented by any further written communications between Mahler and Adler. In 1906 Adler apparently heard Mahler's Sixth Symphony in Vienna, but no particulars have been discovered about further contacts. For 1907 Frau Mahler reports a conversation with Adler after the second performance of Schoenberg's Chamber Symphony, Op. 9, at which Mahler had publicly demanded silence from an unruly audience. Adler is quoted as saying: 'Gustav exposed himself terribly today ... it may cost him his job ... you ought to stop him. I went home and wept over the ways of music. Yes, I wept...'[71] Unquestionably Adler was not greatly in sympathy with the direction taken by Schoenberg after the very early works. Mahler himself said that 'I don't understand his music, but he's young and perhaps he's right. I am old and I daresay my ear is not sensitive enough.'[72] Yet if the above episode is accurately reported, Frau Mahler, as in most of her few references to Adler, fails to balance her account of the historian's over-anxiety at this moment with any glimpse of his genuine help at other times. Nor does she give any glimpse of his support for Schoenberg only two years earlier.[73] Such references and omissions suggest that by this time Frau Mahler, whether consciously or unconsciously, had come to group Adler with those older friends of Mahler whom she admittedly disliked.

Adler later believed that Alma Mahler deliberately tried to separate her husband from his older friends. Frau Mahler explicitly denies any such intention with regard to Adler in a letter probably written in 1909,[74] but the hostility between them is obvious in the letters dating from the years immediately following Mahler's death. What may have led Adler to the conclusion that he reached is uncertain. Unquestionably what turned *him* against Frau Mahler more deeply than any personal slight was his conviction that she was ultimately responsible for Mahler's final determination to leave Vienna and undertake the American voyages that ended in his death. Adler had conceived the plan for Mahler to oversee the Conservatory, and for him it remained a distinct alternative to the American trips, a way in which Vienna could have 'kept Mahler'.[75] In his study Adler takes considerable pains to indicate that Mahler *could* in fact have remained in Vienna; that he was, however, upset by 'influences from another quarter'[76] in addition to the circumstances of his departure from the Court

Opera; and that his earnings in America were required to 'provide a broader material foundation for his family'[77] rather than for his own personal needs. That indeed there was this practical possibility of remaining in Vienna, although Adler seems not to have recognized its psychological impossibility, and that it was actually discussed, is confirmed in two notes to Adler from Dr Max Graf Wickenburg, who had been charged with the reorganization of the music department of the government:

Most esteemed Herr Professor!   Vienna, 18 June 1907
I did not wish to leave behind the accompanying letter yesterday, because it was open, and therefore now permit myself to return it at this point with many thanks.

Hoping soon to be able to report orally to you the details of the discussion with Director Mahler - who personally has now also completely captivated me - I remain, most esteemed Herr Professor, with best regards,
very devotedly, Wickenburg

The following card, although undated, was probably written a short time after that quoted above:

Most esteemed Herr Professor!
Would allow myself to report that, on the day after your friendly visit, with the authorization of His Excellency, I spoke with Director Mahler, who throughout the inquiry seemed very sympathetically moved, but in more detailed discussion explained a number of reasons which unfortunately made the project seem unfeasible to him - at least at present.
With best regards,
most devotedly, Wickenburg

This brief report put an end to Adler's dream of Mahler's continued activity in Vienna. In December 1907, Mahler set off on his journey to the United States. Strains in the friendship, however, are not immediately apparent in the surviving documents. Even Alma Mahler continued to maintain the outward forms of a friendship in which she did not genuinely share. In a letter to Adler dated only a few days after Mahler's initial performance of Beethoven's *Fidelio* at the Metropolitan Opera House on 20 March 1908, she wrote:

24 March
Hotel Majestic, New York
Dear Friend!
Finally I have the time to reply to you. - We live in such a turmoil here

- something else is always going on, and that is very good for us. - The people have responded to G. with open arms. *Fidelio* with the Roller sets was a couple of days ago - and it was an *unprecedented* success. Gustav is just about to sign for next year. On the whole we both feel ourselves immensely well. Not least are we indebted to the dear warm people who all strive to make the stay as lovely as possible for one. We Viennese had no idea of an American winter with its *eternal* sunshine. We will soon be home. Until then we both send warmest greetings to you both.

Alma Mahler[78]

A picture postcard showing Puvis de Chavannes' 'Muses Welcoming the Genius of Englightenment' followed from Boston. It was written jointly by Mahler, his wife and, most probably, the violinist Eugen Grünberg (1854-1928). Grünberg, who had participated in Mahler's concert in Iglau thirty-two years earlier (1876), had emigrated to the United States and eventually become a well-known teacher at the New England Conservatory in Boston.

[postmarked 12 April 1908]

Servus, old man!
   I could not bring myself round to more - and now it is too late, In two weeks I will tell you everything orally. Greetings - Gustav Mahler
Many cordial greetings from me also Alma M.
In old friendship most cordial greetings from your faithful Eugen

Yet another card was written during the return voyage on the *Kaiserin Augusta Victoria:*

[postmarked Cuxhaven, 2 May 1908]
Warmest greetings to you and your dear wife. I am coming to Vienna the middle of May!

Your Gustav Mahler
Many cordial greetings from me, and to a happy reunion!

Alma

The draft of a letter by Adler to a publisher who, although unnamed, can be identified as Oskar von Hase (1846-1921) of the Breitkopf and Härtel establishment, confirms that Adler was in touch with Mahler soon after the latter's return to Vienna. In his draft, dated 31 May 1908, Adler states that Mahler has his Seventh Symphony ready for publication and that, although he has already received other offers, Hase's firm might be interested in exploring the possibility of publishing the work. Plans for the first performance of the symphony in Prague the following September are also noted.

A short letter from Mahler to Adler from the summer of this year shows that nothing came of the attempt to interest Breitkopf and Härtel in the Seventh.

Dear Friend!

I am astonished that you are still in Vienna. It must be unbearable there!

My signature appears on the opposite page. Haase [*sic*] has not written. Most probably he is publishing the complete works of Wallnöfer[79] and Weingartner.[80] –

People of this sort are always the same, I know some specimens of the type.

Here it is glorious! It is too bad that you cannot come for a few days. The first performance of my 7th is now definitely set for the *19th* of September in Prague. I hope definitely to greet you there and remain, with most cordial greetings

Your old Gust. Mahler

My wife sends warmest greetings.

What document may have accompanied this letter that required Mahler's signature is unknown, nor is it certain whether or not Adler was able to attend the performance of the Seventh in Prague. In a letter written in the fall of 1908 to the young composer and historian Egon Wellesz, a student of both Adler and Schoenberg, Mahler sends his regards to Adler and promises to write shortly.[81] No further communications survive, however, until the following spring, when Adler was in the midst of preparations for the Haydn Centennial Festival and the concurrent meeting of the International Musical Society, both of which he organized.[82] And from this time, when Mahler was again in the United States, all that is found is a picture postcard of 'The Times Building' with greetings in Frau Mahler's hand:

[postmarked 2 April 1909]

Many cordial greetings to you both, from both of us.

Alma Mahler
Gustav Mahler

The tensions between Adler and Alma Mahler apparently first came out into the open during the summer of this year. In a letter probably written at this time, but possibly dating from the following summer, she tried to dispel Adler's suspicions:

Thursday

Most esteemed Friend

I have learned that you have the feeling that it might have been my intention to alienate you from Gustav! I am immensely sorry! In this entire year – which is now finally past, I have experienced such terrible oppressiveness – such a chain of sorrows – that I was shy – of every person with whom I had not yet spoken – from fear of losing my laboriously won self-control!! Thus it happened that we seemingly neglected you and your dear wife. I had to tell you this and at the same time assure you that my great respect and truly warm friendship for you and your dear wife has *never* diminished!! – Gustav asks that you definitely visit him here! It is gorgeous here and you would certainly enjoy yourself with us! Warmest greetings to you and your dear wife.

Alma[83]

The last, and perhaps the most interesting, of the previously unknown letters of Mahler to Adler dates from November or December 1909, when Mahler was once more in New York. It is important in a number of respects. Perhaps more directly than any of the currently available letters of the composer, it shows how deliberately and consciously[84] Mahler staked his life on the possibility of surviving the conducting chores of his last years in order that he might ultimately write and work in peace, and at the same time provide his family with the comforts that he felt they deserved. Perhaps he had the example of Richard Strauss in mind. In terms of Mahler's relations with Adler, the letter suggests that they had not in fact seen each other the preceding summer and provides background that is essential for a full understanding of the single letter to Adler already published in the *Briefe*.

Dear Friend!

[I] received your letter this summer in the midst of the turmoil of my departure, which became particularly complicated this time because I gave up my Vienna residence. You will understand that I could not answer you. I did not know my own mind.[85]

Accept warm thanks for your recent indications of life and affection. That kind-hearted (or actually unkind) Löwe did not know what to make of my symphony did not surprise me.[86] It is part of the biography of such a work that in the beginning it is trampled to death by four-square interpreters. Luckily the death is only a seeming one. – This year in the summer I wrote my 9th.

As you can see, I am in quite a hurry. Here real American turmoil prevails. I have daily rehearsals and concerts. Must conserve my strength a great deal, and after rehearsal generally go to bed, where I take my midday meal (here they call the abominable [animal] food 'lunch'). – If I survive these two years without injury – then, I hope, I can also settle down to enjoying everything and perhaps also to creating 'con amore'. It would almost be inappropriate, for actually I should starve and freeze to death with my family somewhere in an attic. This would probably conform to the ideal picture of Hirschfeld[87] and *tutti quanti*. – Now farewell and let me hear from you again. Most cordial greetings to you and your dear wife from me and mine Your

old

Gustav Mahler

That Adler saw this letter as a clear confirmation that Mahler was under a considerable strain, and was not physically well, is hardly surprising. Responding emotionally, he apparently did not conceal his concern from others who were on familiar terms with the composer. He also replied with a letter in which he expressed his feelings directly. This letter has not survived, but the nature of its contents is fairly clear from Mahler's answer. Mahler first tries to allay Adler's worries about his health and then proceeds to justify his American engagement as both an artistic and a financial necessity for himself, and not, as Adler believed, the result of Alma Mahler's demands for a mode of life more luxurious than they could otherwise afford.

The original of this letter is no longer found among Adler's papers. Indeed there is some question as to whether it was ever among them. Its history is the source of a minor mystery, since Adler in commenting on the appearance of the *Briefe* of 1924 carefully noted that he had not received the letter addressed to him in the collection.[88] Yet, curiously, especially in the light of Adler's demonstrable reticence in connection with the publication of private letters, it had already appeared in print in the special Mahler issue of *Der Merker* in 1912, without an indication of its recipient,[89] and a facsimile of one page also had been reproduced in Specht's 1913 volume.[90] When Frau Mahler wrote to Adler while preparing the *Briefe* and asked for his letters, he refused, referring her to the 'New York letter', which she apparently already had in her possession, and which only recently still belonged to her daughter Anna. It is of course possible that Adler, having for some reason allowed the publication of the letter in 1912, did not wish to acknowledge later that it had been addressed to him. It is perhaps more likely that Adler was telling the truth, and that Mahler, having written the letter, decided not to send it. Finding it among his papers after his death, Alma Mahler may then have allowed its publication. We shall probably never be able to determine exactly what happened with any degree of certainty.

The letter is presented here in its entirety, so that it may be seen in relation to its predecessor:

New York, 1 January 1910

Dear Friend!

My last letter seems to have been badly misunderstood by you. I learn this from a quantity of letters that I have been getting from Vienna for several days; and from them it is apparent that most unjust and (I admit it) also vexing interpretations have been linked to it. Thus firstly, *ad vocem* letter: I often go to bed after rehearsals (I first heard of this hygiene from Richard Strauss) because it rests me splendidly and agrees with me excellently. In Vienna I simply had no time for that. – I have very much to do, but by no means too much, as in Vienna. On the whole I feel myself fresher and healthier in this activity and mode of life than in many years. –

Do you really believe that a man as accustomed to activity as I am could feel lastingly well as a 'pensioner'?

I absolutely require a practical exercise of my musical abilities as a counterpoise to the enormous inner happenings in creating; and this very conducting of a concert orchestra was my life-long wish. I am happy to be able to enjoy this once in my life (not to mention that I am learning much in the process, for the technique of the theater is an entirely different one, and I am convinced that a great many of my previous shortcomings in instrumentation are entirely due to the fact that I am accustomed to hearing under the entirely different acoustical conditions of the theater). Why has not Germany or Austria offered something similar? Can I help it that Vienna threw me out? – Further: I need a certain luxury, a comfort in the conduct of life, which my pension (the only one that I could earn in almost thirty years of directorial activity) could not have permitted. Thus it was a more welcome way out for me that America not only offered an occupation adequate to my inclination and capabilities, but also an ample reward for it, which soon now will put me in a position to enjoy that evening of my life still allotted to me in a manner worthy of a human being. And now, most closely connected with this situation, I come to speak of my wife, to whom you with your views and utterances have done a great injustice. You can take my word for it that she has nothing other than my welfare in view. And just as, at my side in Vienna for eight years, she neither allowed herself to be blinded by the outer glamour of my position, nor allowed herself to be seduced into any luxury, even one quite appropriate to our social position, in spite of her temperament and the temptations to do so from Viennese life and 'good friends' there (who all live beyond their circumstances), so now also her earnest endeavor is nothing but to put a quick end to my exertions (which, by the way, I repeat, are not over-exertions, as in Vienna) for my independence, which should make it possible for me to create more than ever. You certainly know her well enough! When have you noticed extravagance or egotism in her? Do you really believe that in the time recently that you have no longer seen each other she has changed so very suddenly? I like to drive a car as much as (indeed much more than) she. And are we perhaps obligated to eat the charity bread of the Vienna Court Opera in a garret in Vienna? Should I not, inasmuch as it is offered me, in a short time earn a fortune in honorable artistic work? Once more I assure you that to me my wife is not only a brave, faithful companion, sharing in everything intellectually, but also (a rare combination) a clever, prudent steward, who, without regard for all the comfort of bodily existence, helps me put by money, and to whom I owe well-being and order in the true sense. I could amplify all this with figures. But I think that is unnecessary; with some good will (and remembrance of past impressions), you will be able to say everything yourself. – Forgive my scrawl and attribute my prolixity to the regard and friendship I preserve for you, and to the wish that you will not inflict a grievous injustice upon my wife, and hence upon me also, through misunderstanding of an expression in my letter.

Most cordial greetings to you and your family from
Your Gustav Mahler

In spite of its sharply critical tone, this letter, together with its predecessor, provides the most convincing evidence of the closeness of the friendship between Mahler and Adler. From them it is clear that both men could and did express themselves with the greatest directness in fundamental and sensitive areas. Yet even in basic disagreement, the friendship survived. Mahler seems to have understood that only genuine concern motivated what, in this case, would seem meddling in his personal affairs. Clearly Adler misunderstood or misjudged the relationship between Mahler and his wife. In his study the historian perceptively noted that, in spite of an occasional lack of restraint, Mahler's 'clear intellect was also master of the final consequences of his actions'.[91] Yet he did not seem to have realized that, in this case also, it was Mahler, not his wife, who had made the fundamental decision and that he was indeed aware of the potential consequences of his actions. In these letters one also senses, however, that Mahler, having decided to risk everything, to live or die for Alma, was no longer willing to consider the genuine alternatives that Adler pressed on him.

Although these letters are the last that Mahler is known to have written to Adler, the exchange did not mark the end of their friendship. On Mahler's brithday, 7 July 1910, Adler offered a public statement of his love and esteem in the article 'G. M. Zum

50ten Geburtstag, Ein Freundeswort' in the *Neue freie Presse* (also included in *Gustav Mahler, ein Bild der Persönlichkeit in Widmungen,* edited by Paul Stefan and published the same year).[92] His continuing anxiety about Mahler is reflected in one statement in particular: 'I have only a single wish: that I, the elder, may not live to see your work finished before me!'[93] His apparent fear that this would be the case was all-too-well founded. From the unpublished *Nachwort* mentioned earlier, it is clear that the two men met and discussed Mahler's Eighth Symphony and that Adler attended the première of the work in Munich on September 12.[94] But Adler's intense feelings about Mahler's repeated trips to the United States did not change and later gained expression in this afterword. There, with the frustrated grief that grew out of witnessing a tragedy that he felt could have been averted, he reviewed their final contacts:

[This Essay] was the result of long preparatory work and study, as well as the accompaniment of Gustav Mahler's life from his youth to his grave, [i.e.] insofar as in the very last years (from the time of his American trips) his most immediate circle, which in a manner incomprehensible to me claimed its domestic right to his isolation, especially from old-established friends, permitted more extended communication. No estrangement ever entered into our hearts, our inmost beings. Even before the day of his last, disastrous voyage to America – how his most intimate friends shuddered at the prospect of it, with what grief they saw him depart into the land that could bring him none of the genuine, artistic joy that he longed for, into which the almost mortally exhausted man was driven by others for the sake of the mammon that he scorned – he came to me, pale, with weary eyes, and spoke the words, incomprehensible to me at the time: 'Whatever may happen or put itself between us, we remain old friends in our inmost relations.' Nothing took place, at least nothing that might have estranged him from me. But from sure signs, which I could not unravel until later, influences may well have increased that were aimed at his spiritual separation from the 'old world', and were intended to lead to the luxuriant mode of life of the 'new world' and new, something less than sympathetic, circles. The mortally weary man came back mortally ill, and his noble soul departed into another world – different from that new one suggested to him. At that time I obtained his promise: 'Gustav, you must never again go to America.' He promised, and kept it, as in life every promise was sacred to him.

The last documents among Adler's papers that date from Mahler's lifetime are two drafts of a letter, dated 25 April 1911, in which Adler invites the unidentified recipients to join in sending a message, prepared by the noted literary critic Hermann Bahr (1863-1934), by telegram to Mahler in Paris.

After Mahler's death, Adler continued to demonstrate the same devotion to his friend that he had shown him in life. His first task, undertaken within a year of the composer's death and completed in 1913, was the memorial essay that forms the first part of this volume. The manuscript of this essay, together with some of Adler's notes and a number of documents obtained in the course of its preparation, is still found among the historian's papers. These materials throw some light on the way Adler worked and on the limitations of his study. What is perhaps most obvious is that Adler had not kept systematic factual records connected with the course of Mahler's career beyond those of the types already cited. As a conscientious historian he was also unwilling to trust to his own memory with regard to specific dates and events. Thus he reviewed all the available volumes (Stefan, Schiedermair, Nodnagel etc.), articles, analytical guides and newspaper criticisms that he could locate. In addition, he made written inquiries to check material and to locate further information. Some of his sources are indicated in a note that appeared at the end of the original publication of the essay but was omitted when the work appeared in book form:

The dates that form the basis of the chronological survey in the preceding essay are partially based on the writing of P. Stefan, revised and confirmed as fully as possible in accordance with communications from the management of the Imperial and Royal Theaters in Vienna (conveyed by *Hofrat* von Horsetzky and *Regierungsrat* A.J. Weltner), from the *Generalmusikdirektor* Bruno Walter (Munich), Frau Justine Rosé (Vienna), Dr Béla Diósy (Budapest), Universal Edition (Director Hertzka) and *Lektor* Hans Daubrawa. For their help, the appropriate thanks are here tendered.

The reliance on Stefan indicated in this statement explains a number of similarities in the works of the two men and suggests clearly that specific factual details of Adler's study must be approached with care. Adler's personal contacts with Mahler are reflected primarily in his essential view of the composer as a human being and artist, and only rarely in specific data, for which he largely relied on others;[95] and it is his view of Mahler that still makes the essay worth reading, in spite of errors of the type noted earlier.

Although Adler was aware of the factual limitations of his work, one should not assume that he was unconcerned about them. The following documents among his papers show some of the areas that he checked, and may still be of interest to students of Mahler:

(1)   A brief letter from the composer Robert Fuchs (1847-1927) con-
      firming the fact that he had been Mahler's harmony teacher.

(2)   A letter from the Gesellschaft der Musikfreunde reviewing the sur-
      viving records of Mahler's years at the Conservatory.

(3)   Two pages by Mahler's sister Justine Rosé apparently replying to
      specific queries by Adler about a variety of factual points.

(4)   A four-page manuscript outline of Mahler's activity at the Court
      Opera in Vienna, including a list of new works presented and re-
      cords of performers engaged and dismissed during Mahler's
      tenure, prepared by A. J. Weltner. A portion of a similar list by
      Weltner is reproduced by Specht in his large Mahler study of
      1913.

(5)   A list of performances of Mahler's symphonies.

(6)   A manuscript report, 'Gustav Mahler in Budapest' (five legal-size
      pages), by Dr Béla Diósy, an editor of a Budapest newspaper who
      had direct contacts with Mahler.

In addition, after the essay first appeared, Adler received at least two letters that included corrections:

(1)   A letter from a lawyer in Prague, Dr Gustav Haas, providing de-
      tails about Mahler's engagement in that city, obtained from
      Sigmund Neumann, the nephew of Angelo Neumann.

(2)   A letter from Mathilde Gotthelft, indicating that the Münden
      music festival actually took place in Kassel in 1885.[96]

The surviving printed scores of Mahler's works found in that portion of Adler's library acquired by the University of Georgia do not bear any markings or annotations by Mahler, except perhaps one mentioned by Adler in a later address on Mahler: a double bar indication of the recapitulation in the first movement of the Eighth with which Mahler drew attention to his 'strict observance of sonata form'.[97]

In 1920 Adler was invited to attend the notable Mahler Festival in Amsterdam as an honorary guest. The occasion marked the beginnings of a *rapprochement* between the artists of previously-opposed European countries, and many distinguished figures were present. Prior to the event, Adler helped to publicize it with an article in *Musikblätter des Anbruch*.[98] While there he delivered a brief address, 'Gustav Mahlers Persönlichkeit', subsequently published in the volume of *Vorträge und Berichte* for the festival, edited by C. Rudolf Mengelberg.[99] In this work Adler summarized the view of Mahler that he had already presented in his study, but with a few additional details, such as the reference to the Eighth Symphony noted above. While in Amsterdam he also kept a brief diary (unpublished) in which he jotted down a few random impressions. These show, in addition to a highly favorable reaction to the performances (he credits Mengelberg with finally making the essential character of the Fifth clear to him), a preoccupation with the flagrant wealth and prosperity of Holland in comparison with the terrible poverty of that time in his homeland. After the festival he wrote a brief report for the *Zeitschrift für Musikwissenschaft.*[100]

The badly-strained relations between Adler and Mahler's widow continued for more than a decade after the composer's death and were reflected in Adler's previously-noted refusal to supply material in his possession when Frau Mahler prepared her 1924 collection of her husband's letters. It is ironic that the single letter to Adler included in the volume[101] is the only one that shows serious friction between Adler and Mahler, and that Frau Mahler was the source of that friction. It is doubly ironic, if Mahler did not actually send it. Adler may have been aware of the irony, but other factors also may have entered into his decision not to allow publication of what he had, such as the references in earlier letters to Löwe and Weingartner, who were still alive, and the need to explain the circumstances connected with many of the others. Whatever the reasons, it is regrettable that Adler did not, as did Friedrich Löhr,[102] at the time make all of his letters available with detailed commentary.

The rupture between Alma Mahler and Adler was finally bridged in the years immediately following the publication of the *Briefe.* In a meeting of 29 November 1926, the Gustav Mahler Monument Committee (Gustav Mahler Denkmal Komitee) was formed. As Frau Mahler notes, the characteristically Austrian idea of erecting a monument in memory of the deceased musician was Adler's.[103] She was asked, however, and agreed, to serve on the executive committee of the organization. Through their work together on this project she and Adler re-established a co-operative relationship, if not a close friendship. The long and constantly thwarted efforts of this group to achieve its goal ended in 1939 with the confiscation by the Nazi-controlled government of the money that had been raised.[104]

In one further area Adler also contributed to the perpetuation of his friend's memory: through his work as a teacher. The first doctoral study devoted to an aspect of Mahler's work, Fritz Egon Pamer's study 'Gustav Mahlers Lieder' (1922, abridged publication 1929-30),[105] was done under Adler at the University of Vienna. After Adler's retirement, two of the three remaining dissertations on Mahler done before the Second World War, those of Heinrich Schmidt[106] and Hans Tischler,[107] also came from the same institution. Although the idea that Mahler's music was a suitable subject for serious study had been slow in gaining approval in academic musical circles, the foundations for a broader acceptance were laid in the decades between the two World Wars. If we must be grateful for all that was done by musicians and writers on music during those years, we also inevitably think of all that might have been done that was not.

If, in reviewing the relationship between Adler and Mahler reflected in the documents presented here, one is left with many unanswered questions and with regrets that a richer body of materials has not been preserved, what remains nevertheless provides a deeper insight into Adler's continued and unselfish devotion to Mahler as an artist and human being, from at least the composer's twentieth year until his death and afterward.

APPENDIX

ADDITIONAL NOTES FROM MAHLER AMONG ADLER'S PAPERS

Because of their brevity and, in most cases, the ambiguity of the references made, the following notes add little to the picture of the relationship between Adler and Mahler presented earlier. They are included here for the sake of completeness and for the assumed intimacy that they suggest. Although it is not possible to date each item specifically, certainly the last three, and probably all five, belong to the period from 1897 to 1907. The first two are written on a Viennese brand of paper, the third on a card with the heading 'K. u. k. Direction des k. k. Hofoperntheaters', the fourth and fifth on cards with the heading 'Der Director des k. k. Hofoperntheaters'. The nature of the 'expositions' and the 'supply' (both rather ambiguous terms in the original German texts) in the first two, and of the contents of the accompanying letters in the third and fifth, must remain matters for speculation.

(1) Dear Friend!
  Am done again: have read your expositions with great interest. Splendid! The continuation, please!
                    Most cordially your
                                          M.

(2) Dear Friend!
  I am done with the present supply! The continuation, please! Here everything is the same as ever, and we - wait!
                    Most cordial greetings
                                          M.

(3) Dear Friend!
  The enclosed for friendly information. What and how should I answer?
                    Most cordially your
                                          G. M.

(4) Dear Friend!
  Why don't you let me hear anything from you? - Do come by - I cannot come to you, since I am up to my neck in work,
                    Most cordially your
                                          Mahler

(5) Dear Friend!
  The enclosed letter for your information and - expert opinion! What do you think of my answer? I hope to see you soon.
                    Most cordially your
                                          M.

117

CHRONOLOGICAL TABLE

7 July 1860

Born in Kalischt (Kaliště), Bohemia, on the Moravian border, as second-eldest child.

Parents: Bernhard Mahler and Marie Mahler (née Hermann).

Father, distiller and liquor dealer, born in Lipnitz (Lipnice) 2 August 1827, died in Iglau (Jihlava) 18 February 1889.

Mother, born 2 March 1837 in Leddetsch (Ledeč), died 11 October 1889 in Iglau.

Brothers and sisters: Isidor, born 22 March 1858, died accidentally the following year.

Ernst, born 1861, died 13 April 1875.

Leopoldine, born 18 May 1863, married Ludwig Quittner, died 27 September 1889.

Karl, born August 1864, died 28 December 1865.

Rudolf, born 17 August 1865, died 21 February 1866.

Louis (Alois), born 6 October 1867, died in the 1920s in the United States.

Justine, born 15 December 1868, married the violinist Arnold Rosé in 1902, died in 1938.

Arnold, born 19 December 1869, died 15 December 1871.

Friedrich, born 23 April 1871, died 14 December 1871.

Alfred, born 22 April 1872, died 6 May 1873.

Otto, born 18 June 1873. Became a musician. Committed suicide 6 February 1895.

Emma, born 19 October 1875, married the violoncellist Eduard Rosé in 1898, died 15 May 1933.

Konrad, born 17 April 1879, died 9 January 1881 of diphtheria.

October 1860

Mahler family moves to Iglau, in Moravia, 22 miles (35 km) from Kalischt. There Gustav receives his first introduction to music from Heinrich Fischer, *Musikdirektor* of the Stadtkapelle. At about the age of five he begins lessons on the piano, studying with a series of teachers that includes Jakob Sladky, the theater *Kapellmeister* Franz Viktorin, Johannes Brosch and Wenzel Pressburg.

c. 1866	Attends elementary school and, from 1869 to 1875, the Gymnasium in Iglau (in Prague, winter semester only, in 1871/2).
c. 1867?	Earliest reported composition: a 'Polka mit einem Trauermarsch als Einleitung' ('Polka with a Funeral March as Introduction'), probably for piano.
October 1870	First documented public performance.
April 1875	Death of brother Ernst, to whom Mahler was strongly attached.
1875-1878	Attends Conservatory of the Gesellschaft der Musikfreunde in Vienna. Piano: Julius Epstein. Harmony: Robert Fuchs. Counterpoint and composition: Franz Krenn. Director: Josef Hellmesberger, Sr. Completes studies, with honors, July 1878. Gymnasium studies continued privately; completed in Iglau in September 1877. Summers generally spent wholly or in part in Iglau throughout this period, and thereafter up to the death of Mahler's parents in 1889. Forms friendships with Hans Rott, Anton Krisper, Hugo Wolf and Emil Freund, among others. Joins Wiener akademischer Wagner-Verein in 1877; leaves it in 1879.
1877-1880	Attends lectures on a wide variety of subjects, including philosophy, history, literature, philology and music history, at the University of Vienna. Intimate intercourse with Anton Bruckner, whose lectures on harmony at the University Mahler also sporadically attends. A piano reduction of Bruckner's Third Symphony, prepared by Mahler, published in January 1880 by Bösendorfer (Bussjäger and Rättig).

Of numerous works begun during the period from 1875 (or somewhat earlier) through 1880, only a few survive.

The earliest preserved compositions include:

(1) Fragment of the song 'Es fiel ein Reif in der Frühlingsnacht' (text by F. von Zuccalmaglio, based on a folk-song source). Undated.

(2) Fragment of the song 'Im wunderschönen Monat Mai' (Heine). Undated.

(3) Piano Quartet in A minor. First movement (1876?).

(4) Sketch of the opening of a scherzo for piano quartet in G minor, found at the end of the manuscript in which the A minor movement is preserved.

The earliest surviving complete works include:

(1)   Three Lieder dedicated to Josephine Poisl, a young lady with whom Mahler was in love at the time he wrote them.

   (*a*) 'Im Lenz' (text by Mahler; the song dated 19 February 1880).

   (*b*) 'Winterlied' (Mahler; 27 February 1880).

   (*c*) 'Maitanz im Grünen' (Mahler; 3 March 1880). Later published as 'Hans und Grethe' in the first volume of *Lieder und Gesänge*.

(2)   *Das klagende Lied,* cantata for soloists, chorus and orchestra, with text by Mahler. Begun 1878, first version completed 1880. Revised 1892/3, and again in 1898/9. Published 1899. Instrumentation revised in 1906. 'Waldmärchen', the original first part of this work, was deleted at the time of the first revision.

A considerable number of other compositions were written during this period but were later either lost or destroyed. Some were simply begun and never completed; others continued to occupy Mahler for some years after 1880. Information about many of these works remains sketchy, but a summary list follows:

(1)   Operas. *Herzog Ernst von Schwaben* (before and around 1875; text by Josef Steiner). *Die Argonauten* (1878?-1880?; text by Mahler and Josef Steiner). *Rübezahl* (1879?-1890; libretto by Mahler preserved, but as yet unpublished).

(2)   Portions of several symphonies, dating from about 1876 to about 1883. Among them a Nordic Symphony or Suite.

(3)   Chamber works, including early piano pieces; a Piano Suite (1876?); a Nocturne for 'cello (1875?-1878?); a Sonata for piano and violin (1875?-1876); a variety of Lieder (surviving fragments of two are noted above); movements for at least one Piano Quintet and possibly two (1875?-1876, 1878); movements for a Piano Quartet, possibly related to one of the surviving movements listed above; perhaps a movement for string quartet.

1880	Becomes a member of an informal socialist and vegetarian group that includes Viktor Adler, a physician and later the leader of the Austrian Social Democratic Party, Albert Spiegler (another doctor), the archaeologist Fritz Löhr and the writer Siegfried Lipiner.
May-July 1880	Conductor at the theater in Hall (Upper Austria), with a monthly salary of 30 florins, and an 'honorarium for each performance' of 50 kreutzer.
Fall 1880	Vienna. Gives piano lessons. Intermittent stays in Iglau.
September 1881-March 1882	Theater conductor in Laibach (Ljubljana). Then returns to Vienna.
January-March 1883	Theater conductor in Olmütz (Olomouc).
March-May 1883	Choir director of an Italian season at the Carl Theater in Vienna.
1883	Songs composed before and around this year, and perhaps also several years later, published in 1892 as volume 1 of the *Lieder und Gesänge (aus der Jugendzeit* added later by a publisher).

(1) 'Frühlingsmorgen' (Richard Leander).
(2) 'Erinnerung' (R. Leander).
(3) 'Hans und Grethe' (Mahler). Written in 1880, and originally titled 'Maitanz im Grünen'.
(4) 'Serenade aus *Don Juan*' (Tirso de Molina).
(5) 'Phantasie aus *Don Juan*' (Tirso de Molina). Both 'Serenade' and 'Phantasie' may have been written for performances of Tirso de Molina's *Don Juan* in Leipzig in 1887.

May-June 1883	Probationary period as assistant conductor at the Royal Theater in Kassel.
July 1883	Visit to Bayreuth (*Parsifal*).
August 1883-July 1885	Royal Music and Choral Director at Kassel, subordinate to the *Kapellmeister* Wilhelm Treiber.
November 1883	A *Vorspiel mit Chor,* now lost, written and performed in Kassel on the occasion of the celebration of the fiftieth anniversary of the debut of the actor Karl Häser.
May 1884	Mahler reportedly writes a *Trauerhymne für die Kaiserin Maria Anna,* who died on 4 May. No copy of the work has yet been traced.
June 1884	Writes music for *tableaux vivants* after Joseph Viktor von Scheffel's *Der Trompeter von Säkkingen* (score destroyed in the Second World War). Per-

formed in Kassel and Karlsruhe. At least the principal theme of one part of this work, and perhaps an entire section, is subsequently used in the 'Blumine' movement of the First Symphony.

December 1884   Completes texts for the *Lieder eines fahrenden Gesellen,* inspired by Mahler's love for the singer Johanna Richter. Original version of the musical settings of four of the six texts probably completed the following year.

    (1) 'Wenn mein Schatz Hochzeit macht'.

    (2) 'Ging heut' Morgen über's Feld'.

    (3) 'Ich hab' ein glühend' Messer'.

    (4) 'Die zwei blauen Augen'.

When the first orchestration of the cycle was undertaken remains uncertain. The earliest surviving keyboard version dates apparently from the late 1880s or early 1890s; the earliest surviving orchestral score dates from 1895. Both may have been preceded by earlier versions that have not been preserved and both were supplanted by published versions that differ somewhat from their predecessors and from each other. Both of these last versions were first published in 1897.

April 1885   Orchestrates folk songs for *Das Volkslied,* a 'Poem with songs, choruses and *tableaux vivants*' by S. H. Mosentahl (score destroyed in Second World War).

June 1885   Conducts Mendelssohn's *St Paul* at a music festival in Kassel.

July 1885–   Second conductor, next to Ludwig Slansky, at the
July 1886   German Theater in Prague (manager, Angelo Neumann).

February 1886   Conducts Beethoven's Ninth Symphony and excerpts from *Parsifal* at the repetition of a concert marking the third anniversary of Wagner's death.

July 1886–   Second conductor, next to Arthur Nikisch, at the
May 1888   Neues Stadttheater in Leipzig (managed by Max Staegemann).

Early 1887–   Realizes and arranges the sketches of Carl Maria von
January 1888   Weber's *Die drei Pintos* to create a finished work. Published in 1888 under the title *The Three Pintos, comic opera in three acts by C. M. von Weber, based on the libretto of the same name by Th. Hell, realized dramatically by C. von Weber* [the son] *and musically by G. Mahler, from posthumous sketches and selected manuscripts of the composer.* First performed 20 January 1888 (thereafter in many German cities; in Vienna, 19 January 1889).

Fall 1887 or Winter 1888	Apparently rediscovers or takes a renewed interest in the well-known collection of German folk poetry *Des Knaben Wunderhorn* [*The Youth's Magic Horn*]. *Old German Songs Collected by L. Achim v. Arnim and Clemens Brentano* (first published 1805-8). Within the period from 1887/8 to 1891 composes his first group of nine songs based on texts from this collection. Published in 1892 as volumes 2 and 3 of *Lieder und Gësange (aus der Jugendzeit)*. 2: (1) 'Um schlimme Kinder artig zu machen'. (2) 'Ich ging mit Lust'. (3) 'Aus! Aus!'. (4) 'Starke Einbildungskraft'. 3: (5) 'Zu Strassburg auf der Schanz''. (6) 'Ablösung im Sommer'. (7) 'Scheiden und Meiden'. (8) 'Nicht Wiedersehen!' (9) 'Selbstgefühl'.
Fall 1888	Completes First Symphony, the earliest drafts of which may extend back to 1883 or earlier, but which was principally written in 1888. First performed as a 'Symphonic Poem in Two Parts' on 20 November 1889 in Budapest. Revised in 1893 (and at that time labelled 'Titan'), again in 1896, and finally in 1906. Published in 1899 (omitting the original second movement, subtitled 'Blumine'). Completes initial version of the first movement of the Second Symphony, which is subsequently labeled 'Totenfeier' for a time. Begins sketches for second movement.
October 1888	Becomes Director of the Royal Hungarian Opera in Budapest, with a contract for 10 years (annual salary, 10 000 gulden; *Intendant*, Franz von Beniczky).
1889	Deaths of father (18 February), sister Leopoldine (27 September) and mother (11 October).
1890	Trip to Italy in May. Remainder of summer at Hinterbrühl near Vienna. On 16 December Brahms hears Mahler conduct *Don Giovanni* in Budapest.
March 1891	Leaves the Budapest Opera. *Intendant*: the one-armed virtuoso pianist and composer, Count Géza Zichy. Compensation for release, 25 000 florins. Mahler immediately takes up a new appointment as first conductor of the Stadttheater in Hamburg (manager, Bernhard Pollini).
August 1891	Vacations alone in Denmark, Sweden and Norway.

January-February 1892	Completes a new group of settings of five poems from *Des Knaben Wunderhorn*, for voice and orchestra. This group is titled *Humoresken*. In the following decade ten more settings are composed. Of these 'Urlicht' was subsequently incorporated into the Second Symphony; 'Es sungen drei Engel' was written for the Third Symphony in a version for chorus and soloist and later adapted for solo performance; 'Das himmlische Leben', written as a separate song, was at one time to be included in the Third Symphony but ultimately became the final movement of the Fourth.

   (1) 'Der schildwache Nachtlied' (1892).
   (2) 'Verlor'ne Müh!' (1892).
   (3) 'Wer hat dies Liedlein erdacht?' (1892).
   (4) 'Das himmlische Leben' (1892).
   (5) 'Trost im Unglück' (1892).
   (6) 'Das irdische Leben' (1892).
   (7) 'Urlicht' (piano version possibly written in 1892; orchestrated 1893).
   (8) 'Des Antonius von Padua Fischpredigt' (1893).
   (9) 'Rheinlegendchen' (1893).
  (10) 'Es sungen drei Engel' (1895-6).
  (11) 'Lob des hohen Verstandes' (1896).
  (12) 'Lied des Verfolgten im Turm' (1898).
  (13) 'Wo die schönen Trompeten blasen' (1898).
  (14) 'Revelge' (1899).
  (15) 'Der Tamboursg'sell' (1901).

1-13 published separately in 1899-1900; 14-15 issued in 1905 as part of *7 Lieder* (*aus letzter Zeit* later added by publisher).

Summer 1892	Directs German opera performances at Drury Lane Theater and at Covent Garden in London, then vacations in Berchtesgaden.
Summer 1893	Steinbach am Attersee (as again in the years 1894, 1895 and 1896). Resumes work on Second Symphony.
Summer 1894	Completes Second Symphony, including in it the song 'Urlicht' composed earlier. First performance in 1895 in Berlin. Two-piano reduction published 1895; full score in 1897.
February 1895	Suicide of brother Otto.
Summer 1895	Drafts Third Symphony, including the two song movements, 'O Mensch!' from Nietzsche's *Also sprach Zarathustra*, and 'Es sungen drei Engel' from *Des Knaben Wunderhorn*.

Summer 1896	Completes Third Symphony. Second movement first performed in Berlin in 1896, the whole work in 1902 under Mahler at the *Tonkünstlerfest* of the Allgemeiner Deutscher Musikverein in Krefeld. First published in 1898.
March 1897	Conducting tour. Berlin, Moscow, Munich, Budapest.
May 1897	Becomes conductor at the Imperial and Royal Court Opera in Vienna. July, appointed Deputy of the Director, Wilhelm Jahn. October, appointed Director.
September 1897	Break with Hugo Wolf.
c. December 1897	Receives subsidy from Gesellschaft zur Förderung deutscher Wissenschaft, Kunst und Literatur in Böhmen (Society for the Advancement of German Science, Art and Literature in Bohemia) to help finance the publication of the scores of the First and Third Symphonies.
June-July 1898	Operation to relieve hemorrhages caused by hemorrhoids. Convalesces at Vahrn.
November 1898	Begins first season as conductor of the Vienna Philharmonic.
Summer 1899	Aussee (in the Salzkammergut). Begins work on the orchestral movements of the Fourth Symphony ('Das himmlische Leben', the final movement, had been written seven years earlier).
Spring 1900	Trip to Venice in April. In June conducts the Vienna Philharmonic in a series of concerts at the International Exposition in Paris.
Summer 1900	Maiernigg am Wörthersee (also in the following summers through 1907). Completes the Fourth Symphony. First performance with the Kaim Orchestra in 1901 in Munich. Published 1902.
Winter 1901	In February falls ill. In March undergoes another operation for hemorrhages. Convalesces in Abbazia (Opatija). Resigns as conductor of the Vienna Philharmonic 1 April.
Summer 1901	Begins work on Fifth Symphony. Completes four orchestral songs on texts by Friedrich Rückert.

    (1) 'Blicke mir nicht in die Lieder'.
    (2) 'Ich atmet' einen linden Duft'.
    (3) 'Ich bin der Welt abhanden gekommen'.
    (4) 'Um Mitternacht'.
These four and the last two *Wunderhorn* songs are published in 1905. A fifth song, 'Liebst du um

126   *Gustav Mahler and Guido Adler*

Summer 1901
contd.

Schönheit', written in 1902, with piano accompaniment, and published later (1907). Orchestrated by M. Puttmann after Mahler's death (1916). The entire group is posthumously titled *Sieben Lieder aus letzter Zeit.*

Completes the first, second and fifth of the five *Kindertotenlieder,* also on texts by Rückert. The third and fourth are composed in 1904. First performance in Vienna in 1905. Published 1905.

(1) 'Nun will die Sonn' so hell aufgeh'n'.
(2) 'Nun seh' ich wohl, warum so dunkle Flammen'.
(3) 'Wenn dein Mütterlein'.
(4) 'Oft denk' ich, sie sind nur ausgegangen'.
(5) 'In diesem Wetter'.

1902

9 March, marries Alma Maria Schindler, daughter of the landscape painter Jakob Emil Schindler, stepdaughter of the painter Karl Moll, a prominent member of the *Sezession* movement.

Children: Maria Anna, born 3 November 1902; dies 5 July 1907.

Anna Justina, born 15 June 1904.

Completes draft of Fifth Symphony (completes orchestration the following year and immediately revises it in 1904). First performed in Munich in 1904. Published the same year.

1903   Begins Sixth Symphony.

1904   Completes Sixth Symphony. First performed in Essen at the *Tonkünstlerfest* of the Allegemeiner Deutscher Musikverein in 1906. Published the same year.

Begins Seventh Symphony.

Actively supports the Vereinigung schaffender Tonkünstler in Vienna, an organization that includes Alexander von Zemlinsky and Arnold Schoenberg, as well as other important younger Austrian composers.

1905   Completes Seventh Symphony. First performed in Prague in 1908. Published in 1909.

1906   Drafts entire Eighth Symphony.

1907   Daughter Maria Anna dies. Doctors diagnose that Mahler himself has heart disease.

Completes orchestration of Eighth Symphony. First performed in Munich in 1910. Piano reduction published in 1910; full score in 1911.

Released from directorship of Vienna Court Opera (as a result of a decision of 5 October). On 15 October conducts there for the last time (*Fidelio*).

Winter season 1907-1908	9 December begins first journey to America. Conducts operas of Wagner and Mozart at the Metropolitan Opera House in New York.
Summer 1908	In Altschluderbach bei Toblach (Dobbiaco) – also in the following summers of 1909 and 1910. Drafts the complete *Das Lied von der Erde*. First performed posthumously in Munich, conducted by Bruno Walter. Vocal score published 1911, full score 1912.
Winter season 1908-1909	Second stay in America. Activities similar to those during his first visit.
Summer 1909	Ninth Symphony drafted. First performed posthumously in Vienna in 1912, Bruno Walter conducting. Edition for piano four-hands published 1912, full score 1913.
Winter season 1909-1910	Third stay in America. Conducts reorganized New York Philharmonic Orchestra in forty-six concerts, and leads a few performances at the Metropolitan Opera.
Summer 1910	Drafts five-movement Tenth Symphony, which remains unfinished at the time of Mahler's death. First performance of first and third movements, Vienna, 1924. First facsimile edition published the same year. Performing version of the entire work prepared by Deryck Cooke, 1963. Published 1976.
	Health deteriorates. Crisis in relationship with his wife precipitates brief meeting with Sigmund Freud.
Winter season 1910-1911	Fourth stay in America. Conducts forty-eight of the sixty-five concerts planned for the New York Philharmonic season. 21 February 1911 conducts for the last time. Illness. Beginning of April goes to Paris for treatment, then home to Vienna.
18 May 1911	Dies at 11 o'clock at night, probably as a result of 'rheumatic heart disease with superimposed subacute bacterial endocarditis'.
22 May 1911	Buried at the cemetery Grinzing.

EDITIONS OF MAHLER'S MUSIC

With regard to Mahler's music, a *Kritische Gesamtausgabe* is in the course of publication under the auspices of the Internationale Gustav Mahler Gesellschaft and with the co-operation of the copyright holders of the compositions. Virtually all of the major works have now appeared except for the songs. To date *Das klagende Lied,* Symphonies nos. 1, 2, 3, 4 (all Universal Edition), 5 (C.F. Peters), 6 (C.F. Kahnt), 7 (Bote and Bock), 8, 9, the opening Adagio from 10 and *Das Lied von der Erde* (the last four again Universal Edition) have been published. New editions of the keyboard and orchestral scores of *Kindertotenlieder* in the series have just appeared. The editorial policy established for the edition by its first and principal editor, the late Erwin Ratz, was to present Mahler's final revisions, which were not always incorporated in the editions published during the composer's lifetime, and to correct errors that had previously remained undetected. Although these editions unquestionably represent improvements over earlier ones, the editors have not always been successful in achieving their goals, and the critical apparatus presented in each volume often leaves something to be desired in providing adequate information about what the editor has done and the bases for his decisions. Thus conclusions about some major issues, such as the sequence of movements in the Sixth Symphony, appear inadequately supported on the basis of the available evidence. Questions about Ratz's approach were raised most emphatically, if not always convincingly, by the late Hans Ferdinand Redlich (see his article in *Die Musikforschung,* cited below), who produced his own editions of Symphonies nos. 1, 4, 6 and 7 for Eulenburg Miniature Scores. These, in turn, raise as many questions as they answer. Philharmonia has based its new miniature scores of the symphonies on the critical edition.

The Internationale Gustav Mahler Gesellschaft has also sponsored the publication of facsimile editions of the draft orchestral score of the first three movements of the Ninth Symphony (Universal Edition, 1971) and of the drafts and sketches of the Tenth Symphony (Munich: Walter Ricke; Meran: Laurin, 1967). An earlier, less complete but superbly produced, facsimile of the material for the Tenth Symphony had been previously issued by Paul Zsolnay Verlag in 1924. The late Deryck Cooke's 'performing version' of the draft for the Tenth Symphony, which incorporates clear transcriptions of the principal surviving autographs, was published in 1976 by Faber Music in London and Associated Music Publishers in New York. The rediscovered 'Blumine' movement of the First Symphony has been published separately by Theodore Presser (Bryn Mawr, Pennsylvania, 1968).

The three volumes of *Lieder und Gesänge [aus der Jugendzeit]*, with piano accompaniment, have been reissued periodically by their original publisher, Schott. They are also included in the first three volumes of the *24 Songs* by Mahler published in 1950 by International Music Co. The original published keyboard version of the *Lieder eines fahrenden Gesellen*, which differs in several important ways from the published orchestral score, is also available from International. Miniature scores of the orchestral version can be had from Philharmonia and Eulenburg. Josef Weinberger in 1977 at last published a new voice-and-piano edition of the song cycle, which was brought into line with the orchestral score by its editor, Colin Matthews. Thus performers now need no longer rely on the less-satisfactory, earlier keyboard version. The later songs from *Des Knaben Wunderhorn* may be obtained from Universal Edition in full scores and piano reductions. Miniature scores (2 vols.), excluding the songs that were incorporated in the symphonies, are published by Philharmonia. *Kindertotenlieder* may be purchased in a miniature score from Philharmonia or Eulenburg, and with a keyboard reduction from C.F. Kahnt or International. The *Sieben Lieder [aus letzter Zeit]*, including the five Rückert songs and the last two songs from *Des Knaben Wunderhorn*, are available in a Philharmonia miniature score and in a keyboard reduction from C. F. Kahnt.

The deleted first part of *Das klagende Lied*, entitled 'Waldmärchen', has been issued in full and vocal scores by Belwin-Mills (Melville, New York). The early Piano Quartet movement in A minor, and the sketch for the beginning of another movement in G minor, have been published by Sikorski. Two of the three early songs written for Josephine Poisl in 1880 remain unpublished, as does the libretto for the opera *Rübezahl*.

NOTES

The composer and the music historian: an introduction

1 For information about the facts of publication of this and the following works mentioned in this introduction, see the bibliography.

2 The principal document presently known is a letter of Gisela Tolney-Witt of 7 February 1893, first published in the *Neue Zürcher Zeitung* (10 May 1958, out-of-town edition), and subsequently in the article of P. Nettl, 'Gustav Mahler als "Musikhistoriker"; ein bisher unveröffentlicher [*sic*] Brief des Meisters', *Musica*, 12 (1958), 592-5. A translation is included in *Selected Letters of Gustav Mahler*, ed. Knud Martner (London, 1979), pp. 147-9, and in H-L. de La Grange, *Mahler* (Garden City, New York, 1973), vol. 1, pp. 270-2.

3 La Grange, *Mahler*, vol. 1, p. 272.

4 Carl Engel, 'Guido Adler in Retrospect (1855-1941)', *The Musical Quarterly*, 27 (1941), 396-8.

Gustav Mahler

1 In addition to the factual corrections in the chronological table noted by Adler later in this foreword, a few very slight changes *were* made in the text of the 1916 edition of the study. These are indicated in the notes to the present edition.

2 Richard Specht, *Gustav Mahler* (Berlin, 1913), p. 9. This volume appeared almost simultaneously with Adler's, and Adler did not become familiar with it until after he had completed his own work. In preparing his essay he had, however, studied Specht's brief earlier work, *Gustav Mahler*, Moderne Essays (Berlin, 1905), and his analysis of the Eighth Symphony (Vienna, 1912).

3 Jihlava in modern Czechoslovakia. See Kurt Blaukopf, *Mahler; A Documentary Study*, with contributions by Zoltan Roman (New York, 1976), illustrations 7-13, for pictures of the town when Mahler was a boy and young man. This volume provides valuable visual and written documentary evidence for almost every stage in Mahler's life.

4 The surviving early poems by Mahler are quoted by La Grange, *Mahler*, vol. 1, pp. 824-37. Mahler also wrote the libretto for his projected opera *Rübezahl*, and the texts for the cantata *Das klagende Lied* and his song cycle *Lieder eines fahrenden Gesellen*. Some late poems written for Alma Mahler are included in her *Gustav Mahler, Erinnerungen und Briefe* (Amsterdam, 1940), pp. 459-64. The majority of the latter are omitted in the English translation of the volume.

5 Adler may have judged by more critical standards than those of modern writers on music, but the surviving documentary and musical evidence of Mahler's early training and accomplishment suggests that he was more advanced than Adler indicates here. See La Grange, *Mahler*, vol. 1, pp. 13-26. Mahler's student piano quartet movement also displays considerable skill. But it should be remembered that Mahler himself was dissatisfied with his training and worked to remedy what he considered his own deficiencies, especially in

130

counterpoint, for many years. See Donald Mitchell, *Gustav Mahler, The Early Years,* 2nd ed., rev. and ed. by Paul Banks and David Matthews (London, 1980), pp. 280-7.

6 Josef Hellmesberger, Sr (1828-1893) was Director of the Conservatory of the Gesellschaft der Musikfreunde from 1851 to 1893.

7 Many modern scholars seem to overlook the influence of Beethoven's late quartets on Mahler and certainly this influence is not always obvious. But Mahler's experiments with different over-all patterns of organization in his symphonies, his motivic development, his contrapuntal idiom and even the character of some individual movements, suggest the example of Beethoven's late works. William J. McGrath, *Dionysian Art and Populist Politics in Austria* (New Haven, 1974), pp. 151-2, draws attention to the connection between the finale of the Third Symphony and the third movement of Beethoven's Op. 135. Mahler's continuing interest in these works is reflected in his performances of Op. 95 and Op. 131 in controversial versions for string orchestra when he was conductor of the Vienna Philharmonic. See La Grange, *Mahler,* vol. 1, p. 498.

8 A musical association, generally consisting of or including dedicated amateur performers. Hellmesberger nevertheless apparently refused to perfom a student symphony by Mahler because of mistakes in the orchestral parts. See La Grange, *Mahler,* vol. 1, p. 717, and Mitchell, *Mahler, The Early Years,* pp. 131-2, 303-4.

9 In recent years some attempts have been made to show that conditions at Mahler's earliest posts were not quite as bad as depicted in earlier studies. See, for example, K. Blaukopf, *Gustav Mahler,* trans. Inge Goodwin (New York, 1973), pp. 257-8. In fact Adler's views seem substantiated by the surviving evidence. Whatever the 'objective' conditions, they left Mahler totally dissatisfied in any artistic sense.

10 Editorial emendation: the original text reads 'At the age of twenty-four...'

11 Author's emendation: in the 1914 edition of the text A. Seidl's name is given. This is corrected in the 1916 edition.

12 A national or provincial commission.

13 'Manager in difficulties'. *L'Impresario in Angustie* is in fact the title of an opera by Domenico Cimarosa (1749-1801), first produced in Naples in 1786.

14 Three of Popper's letters to Adler related to this episode survive among Adler's papers at the University of Georgia, and are quoted in my study, pp. 84-5.

15 From the unpublished report of Dr Béla Diósy, cited later by Adler. This manuscript, entitled 'Gustav Mahler in Budapest', is also among Adler's papers at Georgia. Diósy was personally acquainted with Mahler during the Budapest period, and one of Mahler's letters to him, concerning the possibility of returning to Budapest, is quoted in Mahler's *Selected Letters,* ed. Martner, pp. 187-8.

16 This and the preceding quotations are all from the same work of Diósy.

17 Diósy's manuscript is again the source. In mentioning Beniczky, Adler mistakenly gives his first name as Stephan.

18 This story is an abbreviated version of the account given by Diósy. The wording is so similar to that of the account cited by K. Blaukopf, *Mahler: A Documentary Study,* pp. 188-9, from an unsigned article in the *Neues Wiener Journal* of 19 May 1911, that it seems possible that Diósy may have written the article or that he at least knew of it.

19 The reference is to the Breitkopf and Härtel edition of Bülow's letters, published between 1895 and 1908. A translation by Hannah Waller appears in *Letters*

of *Hans von Bülow* (New York, 1931; reprint, 1972), pp. 425-6. For fuller information on Mahler's Hamburg years, see J. B. Foerster, *Der Pilger: Erinnerungen eines Musikers*, trans. P. Eisner (Prague, 1955), and F. Pfohl, *Gustav Mahler, Eindrücke und Erinnerungen aus den Hamburger Jahren*, ed. Knud Martner (Hamburg, 1973).

20 Ludwig Schiedermair, 'Gustav Mahler als Symphoniker', *Die Musik*, 1 (1901-2), 507.

21 The Christian Social Party of Karl Lueger (1844-1910), who skillfully exploited anti-Semitic feeling to achieve some of his political goals. In the original text of the following sentence Adler mistakenly indicated that Mahler had converted to Catholicism 'two years' before he moved to Vienna. Mahler himself was not entirely honest in this matter; he was actually baptized on 23 February 1897 in Hamburg. See K. Blaukopf, *Mahler: A Documentary Study*, p. 209.

22 On the opposition to Mahler in Vienna, see R. Specht, 'Mahlers Feinde', *Musikblätter des Anbruch*, 2 (1920), 278-87. The scurrilous nature of the published attacks may be seen clearly in the passages quoted by La Grange, *Mahler*, vol. 1, pp. 544ff.

23 Specific information on the personnel hired and dismissed from the Court Opera during Mahler's tenure, as well as material on new productions, discussed by Adler below, was provided by A. J. Weltner, the archivist of the institution. The original lists are still found among Adler's papers. Weltner provided the same or very similar material to Richard Specht, who made use of a portion of it in his 1913 volume on Mahler, pp. 375-8. K. Blaukopf, *Mahler: A Documentary Study*, p. 251, provides a list of new works and new productions during Mahler's ten years at the Court Opera.

24 For further information on Mahler's concern for his orchestras, at both Hamburg and Vienna, see La Grange, *Mahler*, vol. 1, pp. 310-11, and 505. At Vienna he also tried to improve conditions for the stage hands. See La Grange, *ibid.* p. 484.

25 Their first work together was *Tristan und Isolde*, produced in 1903.

26 For Roller's own report on Mahler's attitudes toward operatic staging, see 'Mahler und die Inszenierung', *Musikblätter des Anbruch*, 2 (1920), 272-5. Some of Roller's designs are reproduced in Specht's 1913 volume, pp. 27-43 (omitted in later editions of the volume). K. Blaukopf, *Mahler: A Documentary Study*, pp. 233-4, 237-8, provides other valuable contemporary reports about the productions of *Tristan* and *Fidelio*.

27 Volume for the years 1903-4, pp. 267-75.

28 Paul Stefan's *Das Grab in Wien: eine Chronik 1903-1911* (Berlin, 1913), provides one of the best contemporary views of Mahler's career in Vienna in relation to other sides of the cultural life of the city.

29 That of Felix Weingartner is referred to. For his side of the story, see *Buffets and Rewards: a Musician's Reminiscences*, trans. M. Wolff (London, 1937), pp. 258-60.

30 The full text of this letter appears, in a different translation, in Mahler, *Selected Letters*, pp. 304-5

31 See Max Burckhard, 'Der Fall Mahler als Politicum', in *Gustav Mahler, ein Bild seiner Persönlichkeit in Widmungen*, ed. P. Stefan (Munich, 1910), pp. 44-50.

32 Adler was convinced that Alma Mahler was responsible for Mahler's decision to undertake the American engagements. See my study, pp. 104-5.

33 Baron Albert Rothschild. See La Grange, *Mahler*, vol. 1, pp. 575-6, and K. Blaukopf, *Mahler: A Documentary Study*, illustrations 182-6 and pp. 223-4.

34 When Mahler suffered a hemorrhage in 1901 and took a sick-leave, the mem-

bers of the Philharmonic took advantage of the occasion to replace him as their conductor with Josef Hellmesberger, Jr. Mahler, however, demanded a *unanimous* re-election for himself for the following season, knowing well that he would not get it.

35 Adler heard Liszt, Rubinstein and Hans von Bülow, and provides an interesting comparison of the three in his *Wollen und Wirken* (Vienna, 1935), pp. 41-3. It clearly contradicts La Grange's reference, *Mahler*, vol. 1, p. 882, note 31, to 'the conventional and traditional ideas of the musicologist', as does this and the following passage in the present work.

36 The full text of Mahler's statement is included in P. Stefan, *Gustav Mahler, A Study of His Personality and Work*, trans. T. E. Clark (New York, 1913), pp. 49-51, in La Grange, *Mahler*, vol. 1, pp. 557-8, and in K. Blaukopf, *Mahler: A Documentary Study*, pp. 221-2. La Grange also reproduces a photograph of the original statement in his illustration 51. A copy of Mahler's score of the Ninth Symphony, with numerous markings indicating the changes that he made, is now on deposit from Universal Edition in the Stadtbibliothek in Vienna; another copy is found in the Anna Mahler bequest at the University of Southampton; and another printed score, which belonged to Arnold Schoenberg and reportedly preserves his copy of Mahler's alterations, is found at the Arnold Schoenberg Institute at the University of Southern California in Los Angeles.

37 For re-examinations of Mahler's work on *Die drei Pintos*, see John Warrack, *Carl Maria von Weber*, 2nd ed. (New York, 1976), pp. 256-72; Herta Blaukopf, 'Eine Oper "Aus Weber"', *Österreichischer Musikzeitschrift*, 33 (1978), 204-8; and the notes by Jack Diether for the recording of the opera made in Munich in 1976 and issued in the United States the following year as RCA album PRL3-9063.

38 Editorial emendation: Adler originally indicated the time parenthetically as 'fourteen days'. Although the work was done quickly, it may have been spread over almost a year, if one counts the first tentative steps.

39 Adler's own parentheses.

40 Source of quotation untraced. It may be a stock legal expression of the day. Adler probably spoke directly with Freund, with whom he was acquainted, when he was preparing his book.

41 Mahler was appointed to the board in 1898. On his connections with the series, see pp. 93, 98-9.

42 On Mahler's relations with Wolf after the former had returned to Vienna, see Frank Walker, *Hugo Wolf*, 2nd ed. (New York, 1968), pp. 435, 440-1, 443, 447-8.

43 Rott died insane on 23 June 1884. See La Grange, *Mahler*, vol. 1. p. 81. Further information on Rott's surviving compositions is found in Leopold Nowak, 'Die Kompositionen und Skizzen von Hans Rott in der Musiksammlung der Österreichischen Nationalbibliothek', in *Franz Grasberger zum 60. Geburtstag*, ed. G. Brosche (Tutzing, 1975), pp. 273-340, and in the dissertation of Paul Banks, 'The Early Social and Musical Environment of Gustav Mahler' (University of Oxford, 1979).

44 Many of the people mentioned here have left some form of written testimony of their admiration for Mahler. About half contributed to Stefan's *Gustav Mahler, ein Bild* cited in note 31 above. The important early Mahler bibliographies of Otto Keller and Arthur Seidl in *Die Musik*, 10, 18 (June 1911), 369-77 and 10, 21 (August 1911), 154-8, provide useful additional information. The relations between Mahler and Richard Strauss are now more fully documented with the publication of their correspondence in *Gustav Mahler and*

Richard Strauss, *Briefwechsel 1888-1911*, Bibliothek der Internationalen Gustav Mahler Gesellschaft (Munich, 1980), edited by Herta Blaukopf, who has also provided the volume with an important accompanying essay.

45 Editorial emendations: Adler's text reads 'he returned twice more, after a Philharmonic Society had been formed in New York which gave concerts under Mahler'. Adler consistently indicates that Mahler came to the United States three times, rather than four (the slip may well be psychological in origin, since Adler strongly opposed these trips). Like most European writers, he also did not understand that an existing orchestra had been reorganized for Mahler rather than a new group created. The reorganization took place in 1909, and Mahler conducted the 1909/10 season and part of that for 1910/ 11. See J. G. Huneker, *The Philharmonic Society of New York and Its Seventy-Fifth Anniversary: A Retrospect* (New York, 1917), pp. 23-5. The same work lists the compositions performed during Mahler's tenure as conductor on pp. 76-86. For further details, see also Howard Shanet's *Philharmonic: A History of New York's Orchestra* (New York, 1975), pp. 207-20.

46 Although he does not mention the fact here, Adler was directly instrumental in helping Mahler to obtain the subsidy mentioned. On his roles in this connection, see my study, pp. 87-90. The 'enthusiastic partisan' who sponsored the Second Symphony was Wilhelm Berkan, an industrialist in Hamburg.

47 Dr Wilhelm Ritter von Hartel (1839-1907). On his important role in the cultural life of Vienna in Mahler's day, see Carl E. Schorske, *Fin-de-siecle Vienna: Politics and Culture* (New York, 1980), pp. 237-45.

48 Again Adler does not indicate his own personal involvement. It was he who in 1904 drew up the memorandum. He discusses it more fully in his *Wollen und Wirken*, pp. 97-100. See pp. 100-1, 105 of the present work.

49 The clause beginning 'it conformed...' was added in the 1916 edition of the essay.

50 Alma Mahler is meant. See pp. 104-5, 108 ff.

51 See Carl Hagemann, 'Der Fall Mahler als Kulturtragödie', in Stefan (ed.), *Gustav Mahler, ein Bild*, pp. 51-6.

52 Editorial emendation: the original text reads 'two-fold'.

53 The phrase quoted is Robert Schumann's. See his *Gesammelte Schriften über Musik und Musiker*, ed. F. G. Jansen (Leipzig, 1891), vol. 1, p. 25.

54 Certainly the Vienna Philharmonic is meant.

55 The subtitle *Titan* was first formally added to the symphony for its performance in Hamburg in 1893. It was *not* used in connection with the work when it was first performed in Budapest in 1889.

56 Source of quotation untraced.

57 The reference appears in a review of Mahler's Third Symphony in the *Grazer Tagblatt* of 5 December 1906.

58 From an untitled contribution by Casella in Stefan (ed.), *Gustav Mahler, ein Bild*, p. 89.

59 *Ibid.* p. 93. On Ritter, see La Grange, *Mahler*, vol. 1, pp. 648ff.

60 See Mahler, *Selected Letters*, pp. 212-14, for a translation of the full letter. (The translation here is my own.)

61 Cf. Specht's analysis of the Eighth Symphony cited in note 2 above. H. F. Redlich, *Bruckner and Mahler*, 2nd ed. (London, 1963), p. 216, disagrees with this interpretation. Yet another, quite different, view of the work's structure is found in Hans Tischler, 'Musical Form in Gustav Mahler's Works', *Musicology*, 2 (1949), 231-42. The parallel with Liszt's B minor Sonata is, of course, a very loose one.

62 E. Decsey recounts this episode in his 'Stunden mit Mahler', *Die Musik*, 10, 18 (June 1911), 353-4.

63 Houston Stewart Chamberlain (1855-1927) was a son-in-law of Wagner, and an all-too-ardent admirer of German culture. His *Die Grundlagen des 19. Jahrhunderts* first appeared in 1899-1901 and achieved a considerable success. An interesting glimpse of its anti-Jewish orientation may be seen in a letter of Cosima Wagner, quoted by La Grange, *Mahler*, vol. 1, p. 511.

64 Mahler's First Symphony was performed at the festival arranged by the Verein in Weimar in 1894. According to Mahler, the response was mixed. The reviews were largely negative. The first full performance of the Third Symphony was presented on a program of the Verein in its 1902 festival at Krefeld, and the response marked a turning-point in the public appreciation and awareness of Mahler's works.

65 Mahler's First Symphony was performed in Prague on 3 March 1898. The reception was enthusiastic.

66 In Stefan (ed.), *Gustav Mahler, ein Bild*, p. 2.

67 Source of quotation untraced. In this whole passage it is clear that Adler, a Jew himself, is refuting the more specious types of anti-Jewish criticism directed against Mahler's music. A quite different view of the Jewish elements in Mahler's works is taken by Max Brod in 'Gustav Mahlers jüdische Melodien', *Musikblätter des Anbruch*, 2 (1920), 378-9, and in other later works.

68 Written by Mahler's close friend Siegfried Lipiner, *Der entfesselte Prometheus* (Leipzig, 1876).

69 One suspects that Adler actually means the third movement rather than the second.

70 What passage Adler had in mind in this movement is unclear. Following a passage over an E pedal, the first trumpet at cue 43 briefly shifts between E and D-sharp, but the harmonic level changes at this point. E-flat is suggested only briefly at cue 44. The opening bars of the fourth movement of the Third Symphony are suggested as an appropriate substitute example.

71 The 'new theme' in the development of the 'Eroica' is actually an out-growth of material in the exposition. The example is thus even more appropriate in suggesting what happens in Mahler's works.

72 In Stefan (ed.), *Gustav Mahler, ein Bild*, p. 66.

73 Mahler had originally indicated three hammer strokes (with an alternative for one of them) but in revising the symphony eliminated the third.

74 Source of quotation untraced.

75 Adler's statement still contains a basic element of truth, but we now know that a few more early works have been preserved. For a review of lost works, fragments and unpublished early compositions, see the chronological table and the review of the editions of Mahler's music. Recently Paul Banks has suggested that the manuscript of a 'Sinfonisches Praeludium', now in the Nationalbibliothek in Vienna, may be a student work of Mahler. The attribution, however, is by no means certain. See Banks, 'An Early Symphonic Prelude by Mahler?', *19th Century Music*, 3 (1979), 141-9, and Mitchell, *Mahler, The Early Years*, pp. 305-9.

76 Editorial emendation. Adler's text reads: '*Das klagende Lied*, composed at the age of eighteen to twenty years, in 1888 underwent a thorough remodeling through omission of the third part, contraction of the first two parts and shortening of the instrumental interludes and, after a considerable time, a further revision of the instrumentation. Its relationship to the first version cannot be clearly established.' He is clearly wrong about the character of the revisions, and no support has been found as yet for the 1888 date. La Grange,

Mahler, vol. 1, p. 731, has been able to establish from unpublished letters of Mahler that a basic revision took place in 1893, and that further modifications occurred in 1898. A later revision of the orchestration dating from 1906, after the publication of the work, is mentioned by Adler in his chronological table, and has been confirmed by recent research. The deleted *first* part, titled 'Waldmärchen', is preserved in a copyist's manuscript in the Osborn Collection at the Beinecke Library at Yale University and has been published separately in a keyboard reduction and in full score by Belwin-Mills. The original three-part version is discussed by La Grange, *Mahler*, vol. 1, pp. 729-38; by Jack Diether, 'Mahler's *Klagende Lied* - Genesis and Evolution', *The Music Review*, 29 (1968), 268-87; and by Donald Mitchell in his introduction to the 1969 American edition of A. Mahler's *Gustav Mahler, Memories and Letters*. In the third enlarged edition (Seattle, 1975), see pp. xxix-xxxiv, and *Gustav Mahler, The Wunderhorn Years* (London, 1975), pp. 56-68.

77 This statement is also made by P. Stefan, E. Decsey and other early writers on Mahler. Decsey, in his 'Stunden mit Mahler', pp. 355-6, specifically mentions having heard the statement from Mahler himself. Mahler's memory may have been faulty, as it was on other occasions, or the implication may be that Mahler first thought of writing an opera but, when he actually got to work, decided on a cantata. Textually the work is certainly not conceived for the stage, although musically there are a number of operatic echoes.

78 These songs originally appeared, as the first volume of three, with the title *Lieder und Gesänge*. The first volume was not published in 1885, as originally indicated by Adler, but in 1892, together with two later volumes containing nine songs on texts from *Des Knaben Wunderhorn*. Sometime after 1900, when the songs were temporarily issued by Universal Edition, the phrase *aus der Jugendzeit* was added in brackets on the cover, to distinguish them from the later songs. They are generally known with this addition today. See Mitchell, *Mahler, The Early Years*, p. 199.

79 See 'Mahlers Weg. Ein Erinnerungsblatt', *Der Merker*, 3, 5 (March 1912), 166-71. In his later book on Mahler, however, Walter, like most other writers on Mahler, treats *Das Lied von der Erde* and the Ninth Symphony as belonging to a separate style-period. To this period we would now also add the Tenth Symphony.

80 The question of when Mahler became acquainted with the *Wunderhorn* texts is a subject of debate. Mitchell, in the introduction to his revised edition of A. Mahler's *Gustav Mahler, Memories and Letters*, p. xxiv, indicates that there is 'ample evidence to hand that suggests that it would have been virtually impossible for him *not* to have been familiar with the *Wunderhorn* anthology long before 1888'; and one of the texts of the *Lieder eines fahrenden Gesellen* of 1884-5 is clearly derived from a *Wunderhorn* poem. K. Blaukopf, *Gustav Mahler*, pp. 72-4, suggests that this relationship may stem from actual knowledge of the songs rather than the collection. And R. Specht, in his chronology of Mahler's life (in the analysis of the Eighth Symphony cited earlier), reports that between 1864 and 1866 Mahler 'already sings over 200 folk songs, which he learns from the maid'. Mahler's own statements are contradictory. It seems likely to me that Mahler had in fact come to know the collection and at least some of the poems in it in his earlier years, that subsequently it slipped his mind, and that in 1887-8 he rediscovered the volume. This view, however, is only an hypothesis and does not entirely resolve certain questions.

81 Adler's statement is somewhat misleading, since Mahler's heart disease had been diagnosed before these two works were written, and he clearly sensed the possibility of his death.

82 See A. Casella, 'Gustav Mahler et sa deuxième Symphonie', *S. I. M. Revue musicale mensuelle*, 6, 4 (15 April 1910), 250, and W. Ritter, 'La neuvième de Gustave [*sic*] Mahler', *S. I. M. Revue musicale mensuelle*, 8, 7-8 (July-August 1912), 41-7. Adler probably picked up Casella's point of view from Stefan's study. Casella actually indicates that Mahler *himself* had suggested this stylistic division. As stated earlier, most later writers disagree with Adler on this point.

83 Exactly which songs Adler had in mind is not certain. He probably refers to the remaining orchestral songs from *Des Knaben Wunderhorn*, including 'Revelge' and 'Der Tamboursg'sell', and, from the 'Rückert' songs, 'Um Mitternacht'.

84 Somewhat different totals are arrived at depending upon whether one counts the unpublished early songs and all of the songs included in the symphonies, some of them, or none.

85 Editorial emendation. Adler's text reads: 'The five songs are based on a fundamental motive ($a^2 g^2 c^2$)...' From underlinings in Adler's copy of J. V. von Wöss' thematic analysis of *Das Lied von der Erde* (Vienna, 1912), it is clear that a g e was intended, and that the other slips, here and below, concerning the number of movements and who sang them, were inadvertent howlers.

86 Editorial emendation. Adler's text reads 'two'.

87 Editorial emendation. Adler's text reads 'four'.

88 'Give light to our senses, pour love into our hearts.'

89 This subject is perhaps most fully explored in Heinrich Schmidt's unpublished thesis, 'Formprobleme und Entwicklungslinien in Gustav Mahlers Symphonien' (University of Vienna, 1929). Paul Bekker's *Mahlers Sinfonien* (Berlin, 1921), the separate thematic analyses of the symphonies by various authors in the Musikführer series, as well as the guides by R. Specht, are also useful. La Grange, *Mahler*, vol. 1, pp. 712-823, provides introductory analyses of works through the Fourth Symphony, but these must be used with caution. Mitchell's *Mahler, The Wunderhorn Years* contains many stimulating insights into the curious patterns in which the first four symphonies emerged. For further studies of some of the individual symphonies, see the bibliography.

90 A typescript list of performances of Mahler's symphonies through April 1913, found among Adler's papers, forms the basis for these figures. A careful review would modify them slightly but would not alter the picture of the relative popularity of the symphonies up to the time that Adler's study was written.

91 Editorial emendation. Adler's text reads 'twenty-one' here, but in enumerating the performances of the Eighth Symphony below he mentions a total of twenty-two.

92 Unknown to Adler at the time he wrote these lines, Mahler had already drafted a no-less-moving concluding movement for his Tenth Symphony at the time of his death. The final cadence is to an equally clear major triad. The last page of the manuscript includes the lines 'Für Dich leben! Für Dich sterben!' 'Almschi!' ('To live for you! To die for you! Almschi! [i.e. his wife Alma]').

At the conclusion of the 1914 edition of this essay, Adler includes a brief summary of information about editions of Mahler's music, bibliography, visual representations of Mahler and persons consulted to check material. The last of these sections is quoted in my study, p. 113. More extensive information on editions, books and articles is included in the bibliography for the present volume. With regard to visual material Adler notes the existence of the bronze bust by Auguste Rodin, the etching by Fritz Erler, a picture by Emil Orlik, the death mask taken by Karl Moll, twenty-two silhouettes by Otto Boehler, and, among the caricatures, singles out those of Oskar Garvens and Lindloff.

Published photographs he indicates may be found in *Die Musik*, 1, 7 and 17; 4, 4; 5, 16; 7, 9 and 15; and 10, 18. In the 1916 edition of the essay a portrait plaque by Alfred Rothberger is added to the works cited.

Mahler and Guido Adler

[1] Questions about the character of the relationship between Mahler and Adler are raised most specifically by Mitchell in his *Mahler, The Early Years*, pp. 91-3 and note 35, p. 249.

[2] *Biographisches Jahrbuch und deutscher Nekrolog*, 16 (1914), 3-41.

[3] See above, p. 16.

[4] See, for example, the emended passages in the translation, pp. 66, 68 above.

[5] Stefan acknowledged Adler's help in the German edition of his 1910 study of Mahler, but this passage was deleted from the American translation.

[6] See A. Mahler, *Gustav Mahler, Memories and Letters*, pp. 49, 112 and 243. These passages are singled out by Mitchell in the work cited in note 1 above and are discussed in their appropriate contexts in the present study.

[7] See *Recollections of Gustav Mahler*, ed. Peter Franklin, trans. Dika Newlin (London, 1980), pp. 109-10, 166. The full diary of Bauer-Lechner has not been published, but substantial portions of the unpublished sections of the manuscript are cited by La Grange in his *Mahler*.

[8] See, for example, Lipiner's *Über die Elemente einer Erneuerung religiöser Ideen in der Gegenwart* (Vienna, 1878).

[9] For an excellent discussion of the intellectual currents among the younger generations in Vienna in Mahler's day, see McGrath, *Dionysian Art*. McGrath shows clearly that the anti-materialistic and anti-rationalistic directions found in student circles may be seen as a reaction to the Liberal policies that led to the financial crisis of 1873. One chapter of this volume is specifically devoted to Mahler's symphonies (principally the Third).

[10] 'Gustav Mahlers Persönlichkeit', in *Das Mahler-Fest, Amsterdam, Mai 1920: Vorträge und Berichte*, ed. C. Rudolf Mengelberg (Vienna, 1920), p. 17.

[11] *Wollen and Wirken*, p. 3.

[12] *Wollen und Wirken*, p. 6. On Mahler's other teachers, see La Grange, *Mahler*, vol, 1, p. 16.

[13] See, for example, Elsa Bienenfeld, 'Guido Adler', *Die Musik*, 18, 2 (November 1925), 113-28. A copy of this article among Adler's papers has marginal indications of this and other errors. La Grange, although accurate about this point elsewhere, makes the same slip on p. 563 of the first volume of his biography.

[14] *Wollen und Wirken*, p. 4.

[15] See above, pp. 19-20, and *Wollen und Wirken*, pp. 6-8.

[16] *Wollen und Wirken*, pp. 10-11, 'Akademischer' appears in the name of the organization not because it took an academic approach to Wagner, but because the early meetings of the group were held in the well-known Akademisches Gymnasium in Vienna.

[17] See *Siebenter Jahres-Bericht des Wiener akademischen Wagner-Vereines für das Jahr 1879* (Vienna, 1880), pp. 22-6. Why Mahler and his friends left the *Verein* remains an open question.

[18] Schaumann also became *Obmann* of the Akademischer Gesangverein. At one time he wrote a libretto for Hugo Wolf, which the latter did not use. See Adler, *Wollen und Wirken*, p. 12, and Walker, *Hugo Wolf*, pp. 372, 404.

[19] For the original German texts of this and all of the subsequent documents quoted in the course of this study, see the German edition, *Gustav Mahler und Guido Adler, Zur Geschichte einer Freundschaft*, Bibliothek der Internationalen Gustav Mahler Gesellschaft (Vienna, 1978).

[20] The full card is quoted in K. Blaukopf, *Mahler: A Documentary Study*, pp. 165-6. The name 'Adler' also appears in a letter of Mahler to Albert Spiegler (postmarked 12 January 1885), now in the Mary Flagler Cary Collection of the Pierpont Morgan Library in New York. In this letter Mahler sends thanks for New Year greetings to 'Adler, Pernerstorfer and Bondi'. The other names mentioned strongly suggest that Dr Victor Adler (1852-1918), later leader of the Austrian Social Democratic party, is meant.

[21] See Mahler, *Selected Letters*, p. 96. In a subsequent letter Mahler gives the time as from 20 to 24 July.

[22] See above, pp. 20-1. On this concert see also La Grange, *Mahler*, vol. 1, pp. 140-1, and K. Blaukopf, *Mahler: A Documentary Study*, p. 175.

[23] See above, p. 21.

[24] On Mahler's years in Budapest, see K. Blaukopf, *Mahler: A Documentary Study*, pp. 181-90; La Grange, *Mahler*, vol. 1, pp. 182-227; and Alexander Jemnitz, 'Gustav Mahler als kgl. ung. Hofoperndirektor', *Der Auftakt*, 16 (1936), 7-11, 63-7, 183-8. In all of these works, however, the details of how Mahler came to be appointed to the post remain unclear. Certainly other recommendations besides those of Adler and Popper were involved.

[25] Edmund Ödon von Mihalovich (1842-1929). Mihalovich was apparently in charge of a committee designated to select a new Director for the Royal Hungarian Opera. A composer, he was from 1887 to 1919 Director of the Budapest Academy of Music.

[26] The conductor Felix Mottl (1856-1911).

[27] See La Grange, *Mahler*, vol. 1, p. 186.

[28] This information is contained in the letter of Gustav Haas mentioned on p. 114; but Haas apparently confused the work of Cornelius with Rossini's *Barber of Seville*. See La Grange, *Mahler*, vol. 1, p. 182.

[29] Adler is known to have given at least one letter of Bruckner to a collector. Among his papers there are gaps for this same period in his correspondence with some other friends, and in some surviving groups of letters there are indications of damage resulting from dampness.

[30] *Internationale Ausstellung für Musik- und Theaterwesen, Wien 1892: Fach-Katalog der Musikhistorischen Abteilung* (Vienna, 1892). This catalogue shows that Adler himself was at that time already saving some of the letters of his correspondents.

[31] Adler, *Wollen und Wirken*, p. 18. The study was published in 1880.

[32] See above, p. 22. Adler's recommendation, however, was of course only one among many from influential sources. Ludwig Karpath in his *Begegnung mit dem Genius* (Vienna, 1934) traces the complex manoeuvres that led to Mahler's appointment.

[33] Mahler, *Selected Letters*, p. 226.

[34] Bauer-Lechner, *Recollections*, pp. 109-10.

[35] La Grange, *Mahler*, vol. 1, p. 465, gives 21 January as the date of this letter, but in his note to this passage, p. 914, indicates 22 January. The more recent French edition of La Grange's work (Paris, 1979), p. 714, confirms the 21 January date.

[36] In regard to the Second Symphony, the orchestral parts and Bruno Walter's reduction for one piano, four-hands, are probably meant.

[37] At that time this amount was equivalent to 5784 American dollars. It is vir-

tually impossible to estimate an equivalent in present-day currency. La Grange, *Mahler,* vol. 1, p. 475, mistakenly gives the amount as 1200 Gulden, but this passage is eliminated in the revised French edition. The relevant passage from the original document is quoted in K. Blaukopf. *Gustav Mahler: A Documentary Study,* p. 216.

38 Equal to $1446 at the time. There was a single grant of 3000 Gulden, paid in halves, not two separate grants of 3000 each, as indicated by La Grange, *ibid.* The slip is corrected in the French edition, p. 713.

39 The fact *was* mentioned by Stefan, and later in a footnote in the 1924 collection of Mahler's letters.

40 For further details about this concert, see K. Blaukopf, *Mahler: A Documentary Study,* p. 216, and La Grange, *Mahler,* vol. 1, p. 476 and note 4, p. 915. Mahler did not escape a supper in his honor given by Angelo Neumann and attended by Adler, Lipiner and other friends.

41 The first performance of *Donna Diana* took place on 9 December 1898.

42 Mahler actually conducted the *Symphonie fantastique* at a Vienna Philharmonic concert on November 20. Five other brief notes of this type are presented in the appendix at the end of this study; see p. 117.

43 See Theophil Antonicek in his review of the German translation of this study, *Gustav Mahler und Guido Adler,* in *Musicologica Austriaca,* 2 (1979), 161. In the course of his review, Professor Antonicek kindly provides a detailed survey of the surviving documents in the archive (see pp. 160-2 of the review).

44 See above, p. 33.

45 See La Grange, *Mahler,* vol. 1, p. 544.

46 See the review by T. Antonicek cited in note 43 above.

47 See La Grange, *Mahler,* vol. 1, pp. 563-4.

48 See Bauer-Lechner, *Recollections,* p. 166.

49 T. Antonicek, in the review cited in note 43 above, p. 159, suggests the Baron in question may have been Josef Freiherr von Bezecny, who was a member of the board of the Denkmäler. See above, p. 87, and note 62 below.

50 See K. Blaukopf, *Mahler: A Documentary Study,* illustration 184 and p. 223.

51 See above, p. 30. The 'artistic Maecenas' was Baron Albert Rothschild.

52 See La Grange, *Mahler,* vol. 1, pp. 585-6.

53 See above, p. 41. The letter to Seidl is produced in full in Mahler, *Selected Letters,* pp. 212-14.

54 For details, which confirm Mahler's own reservations about his statements to Seidl, see La Grange, *Mahler,* vol. 1, pp. 597-8.

55 Probably a Christmas present.

56 A. Mahler, *Gustav Mahler, Memories and Letters,* p. 30. See also La Grange, *Mahler,* vol. 1, p. 669.

57 A. Mahler, *Gustav Mahler, Memories and Letters,* pp. 25-6.

58 See the appendix, p.117.

59 A. Mahler, *Gustav Mahler, Memories and Letters,* p. 49.

60 All of the unpublished letters of Schoenberg mentioned here are found among Adler's papers.

61 Vol. 5 (1903-4), pp. 267-75.

62 For the date of the meeting, see T. Antonicek in the review of the German translation of this study cited in note 43 above, p. 162. The Bezecny mentioned at the end of this letter is again Josef Freiherr von Bezecny, who was at this time Chairman of the Board of Directors of the Denkmäler der Tonkunst in Österreich. He died later this same year.

63 Issue of 31 March 1904.

64 It should also be noted that many of Schoenberg's followers were students of

Adler. See E. Wellesz, 'Anfänge der "Neuen Musik" in Wien', *Österreichische Musikzeitschrift*, 25 (1970), 312-15.

[65] See above, pp. 34-5. Later, after the Conservatory had been transformed into the K. K. Akademie für Musik und darstellende Kunst, Mahler was in fact made a member of the *Kuratorium*, but the position was merely an honorary one. See P. Stefan, 'Gustav Mahlers Kindheit, erste Jugend und Lehrjahre', *Die Musik*, 10, 18 (June 1911), 344.

[66] See pp. 95-9.

[67] A. Mahler, *Gustav Mahler, Memories and Letters*, pp. 243, 371.

[68] *Ibid.* pp. 259-60, 374.

[69]   15 August 1905

Dear Friend!

My Seventh is finished. I believe this work auspiciously born and well produced. Many greetings to you and yours, also from my wife.

G. M.

[70] Efforts to trace this manuscript have thus far proved fruitless. An important group of sketches for the song is found in the Cary Collection at the Pierpont Morgan Library, and a manuscript with keyboard accompaniment, formerly in the possession of the late Alfred Rosé, is now in the collection of Henry-Louis de La Grange. The autograph full score, however, has not yet been located.

[71] A. Mahler, *Gustav Mahler, Memories and Letters*, p. 112. The implications of the original German text are rather different than those in this translation. Thus I have re-translated this passage.

[72] *Ibid.* Mahler had been so impressed by Schoenberg's First String Quartet, Op. 7, only a few days earlier, however, that he had written to Richard Strauss strongly recommending that the work be included in the programs of the Allgemeiner Deutscher Musikverein at its meeting in Dresden. See Mahler and Strauss, *Briefwechsel 1888-1911*, pp. 122-3.

[73] Frau Mahler apparently continued to suggest that Adler was a dyed-in-the-wool musical reactionary in conversation with other musicians. See Nettl, 'Gustav Mahler als "Musikhistoriker"', p. 593. In fact Adler again lent support to Schoenberg in the period from 1910 to 1913, as is shown by a further group of unpublished letters among the historian's papers. Karpath, in his *Begegnung mit dem Genius*, p. 177, reports an incident that suggests something of Mahler's own perceptiveness with regard to Adler's views. After a performance of one of Mahler's works, the composer, Karpath, Adler and Hans Koessler had dinner together. Koessler, a teacher at the National Academy of Music in Budapest, and Adler became involved in an argument. The next day Mahler reported to Karpath that 'Adler had declared Herr Professor Koessler backward, and that Koessler had said to him that he would never have thought that Adler, whom he considered a solid musician of the good, old school, would go along with the crazy young musicians. "You see" Mahler commented . . . "no one is just to anybody else. Adler is by no means as hyper-modern as Koessler believes, and Koessler in turn is not so reactionary as Adler supposes. In any case it amused me to see them at swords' points. I treasure them both."' La Grange's reference to this episode, *Mahler*, vol. 1, p. 463. misleadingly suggests that Adler and Koessler were quarreling about Mahler's works; Karpath simply says that they were arguing about 'musical questions'.

[74] See p. 108.

[75] See above, p. 35. Adler was quoting the writer Hagemann.

76 See above, p. 35.
77 See above, p. 34.
78 In her *Gustav Mahler, Memories and Letters*, pp. 128-38. Frau Mahler gives a more balanced view of Mahler's first stay in the United States.
79 Adolf Wallnöfer (1854-1944), a singer and composer.
80 Felix Weingartner (1863-1942), Mahler's successor at the Vienna Court Opera. Breitkopf and Härtel did in fact publish many of the compositions of Wallnöfer and Weingartner.
81 E. Wellesz, 'An Unpublished Letter of Mahler', *The Music Review*, 1 (1940), 24.
82 These events were only a fraction of Adler's manifold activities during the period from 1898 to 1911. In addition to the Wagner volume (1904) mentioned in the text, he wrote *Der Stil in der Musik* (1911); completed twenty-eight articles of varying lengths; attended, and actively participated in, a variety of other meetings; founded and directed the Musikhistorisches Institut of the University of Vienna; and edited eight volumes of the Denkmäler der Tonkunst in Österreich.
83 As background for this letter, see Frau Mahler's account of her intense nervousness and her need for a rest cure at Levico during the spring of 1909, in *Gustav Mahler, Memories and Letters*, p. 151.
84 Mahler's heart trouble had been diagnosed in the summer of 1907.
85 Lacking Adler's letter, Mahler's reply is unclear at this point.
86 A performance of Mahler's Seventh Symphony on 3 November 1909, conducted by Ferdinand Löwe (1865-1925), is referred to here. The same performance is mentioned in a letter of Schoenberg reproduced in A. Mahler, *Gustav Mahler, Memories and Letters*, pp. 325-6.
87 Robert Hirschfeld (1857-1914). Originally friendly toward Mahler, he became a bitter critic.
88 See 'Autriche', *Bulletin de la société 'Union Musicologique'*, 5 (1925), 53. The letter appears as no. 416, pp. 461-3 of the *Briefe*. The translation below is my own. For a different version, see Mahler, *Selected Letters*, pp. 348-9.
89 *Der Merker*, 3 (1912), 180-1. A facsimile of one page of the letter also appears among the illustrations found in this volume.
90 p. 61 in the section of illustrations. Specht was indebted to Alma Mahler for many of the illustrations.
91 See above, p. 36.
92 pp. 3-6.
93 *Ibid.* p. 5.
94 David Wooldridge, in his *From the Steeples and Mountains: a Study of Charles Ives* (New York, 1974), p. 206, includes an interesting bit of evidence about the poor state of Mahler's health at the time of the première of the Eighth Symphony in Munich, in the form of a brief extract from the diary of the English music historian Henry Ellis Wooldridge: 'M looks so ill we hardly knew him. Alma says bad heart prognosis poor.' Wooldridge, on pp. 150-1, also produces important evidence that Mahler took the score of Ives' Third Symphony with him to Europe in the spring of 1910 and gave it at least a trial reading in Munich.
95 Specht's analysis of the Eighth Symphony, which contains a chronology of Mahler's life, is also among Adler's papers.
96 Adler's mistake in indicating the location of the festival as Münden was picked up and repeated by many later writers. The work of Hans Joachim Schaefer has established conclusively that the 'Large Music Festival' was at Kassel, with Mahler conducting Mendelssohn's oratorio *St Paul* on 29 June 1885. See H. J.

Schaefer, 'Gustav Mahler in Kassel', in the periodical *informationen* issued by the magistrate of the city of Kassel, June, July/August 1975; February, April, May, June, July/August 1976; February, March, April, May 1977.

[97] Adler, 'Gustav Mahlers Persönlichkeit', in Mengelberg (ed.), *Das Mahler-Fest*, p. 20.

[98] 'Zum Mahler-Fest in Amsterdam', 2 (1920), 255-6.

[99] See notes 10 and 97 above.

[100] 'Mahler-Fest in Amsterdam', 2 (1919-20), 607-8.

[101] See above, pp. 110-11.

[102] Löhr's notes are found on pp. 473-94 of the Mahler *Briefe*. In the translation, *Selected Letters*, they are incorporated in the larger sections of notes prepared by the editor, pp. 385-448.

[103] Alma Mahler Werfel, *And the Bridge is Love* (London, 1958), p. 193. The German edition of this work, published as *Mein Leben* (Frankfurt, 1960), differs considerably from the English version and does not include this passage.

[104] See A. Mahler, *Gustav Mahler, Memories and Letters*, p. lxi. I am indebted to Dr. Carl A. Rosenthal for permitting me to examine the few remaining files of the committee, for which he served as secretary. These documents suggest that a strong element of anti-Semitism was at work to prevent the erection of the monument, and Dr Rosenthal has confirmed this supposition.

[105] *Studien zur Musikwissenschaft*, 16 (1929), 116-38, and 17 (1930), 105-27.

[106] Schmidt, 'Formprobleme und Entwicklungslinien', unpublished dissertation.

[107] Hans Tischler, 'Die Harmonik in den Werken Gustav Mahlers', unpublished dissertation, University of Vienna, 1937. The third dissertation was that of Anton Schaeffer, 'Gustav Mahlers Instrumentation', University of Bonn, 1933. It was published by G. H. Nolte in Düsseldorf in 1935.

BIBLIOGRAPHY

A comprehensive bibliography of the literature about Mahler would now require a separate volume several times larger than the present one. Thus the following list represents no more than a selection of older, and more recent, works which may be of interest to those who wish to explore various facets of Mahler's music and career more fully. I have included in it all of the books and articles that are directly pertinent to the present volume and a cross-section of others representing a wide variety of different topics and points of view. The contents of several Mahler issues of periodicals have been analyzed, and special emphasis has been placed on works containing documentary material. Adequate discussions of Mahler's music still form the smallest segment of the literature on the composer, but that situation is now changing. Those who wish to pursue further research will want to consult the early bibliographies of Otto Keller and Arthur Seidl (see below); the bibliography included in the first volume of the biography of Henry-Louis de La Grange (to which should be added the citations included in his footnotes); and especially the substantial and valuable *Gustav Mahler Dokumentation* by Bruno and Eleonore Vondenhoff published in 1978, which provides a record of the author's rich collection of materials about Mahler, a collection that will ultimately be housed in the Nationalbibliothek in Vienna.

Adler, Guido. 'Autriche', *Bulletin de la société 'Union Musicologique'*, 5 (1925), 50-4.

'"Euryanthe" in neuer Einrichtung', *Zeitschrift der Internationalen Musikgesellschaft*, 5 (1903-4), 267-75.

'G.M. Zum 50ten Geburtstag, Ein Freundeswort', *Neue freie Presse*, 7 July 1910, 7-8. Subsequently republished in Stefan (ed.), *Gustav Mahler*, pp. 3-6.

'Gustav Mahlers Persönlichkeit', in Mengelberg (ed.), *Das Mahler-Fest*, pp. 17-20.

(ed. and contributor). *Handbuch der Musikgeschichte.* Frankfurt am Main, 1924. 2nd ed., 2 vols., 1930. Reprint of 2nd ed., Tutzing, 1961.

Internationale Ausstellung für Musik- und Theaterwesen, Wien 1892: Fach-Katalog der Musikhistorischen Abteilung. Vienna, 1892.

'Mahler-Fest in Amsterdam', *Zeitschrift für Musikwissenschaft*, 2 (1919-20), 607-8.

Methode der Musikgeschichte. Leipzig, 1919. Reprint, Farnborough, Hants., 1971.

'Musik und Musikwissenschaft. Akademische Antrittsrede, gehalten am 26. Oktober 1898 an der Universität Wien', *Jahrbuch der Musik-bibliothek Peters,* 5 (1898), 27-39.

'Eine neue musikalische Vereinigung', *Neue freie Presse,* 3 March 1904. Page numbers unrecorded.

Richard Wagner. Vorlesungen gehalten an der Universität Wien. Leipzig, 1904. 2nd ed., 1923. French trans. by L. Laloy, 1909.

Der Stil in der Musik. Leipzig, 1911. 2nd ed., 1929. Reprint, Walluf, 1973.

Wollen und Wirken, aus dem Leben eines Musikhistorikers. Vienna, 1935.

'Zum Mahler-Fest in Amsterdam', *Musikblätter des Anbruch,* 2 (1920), 255-6.

Adorno, Theodor Wiesengrund. *Mahler. Eine musikalische Physiog-nomik.* Frankfurt, 1960.

'Mahler Heute', *Anbruch,* 12 (1930), 86-92.

Anbruch, [Musikblätter des]. Mahler issues. 2, 7-8 (April 1920) and 12, 3 (March 1930). Individual articles are listed separately by author in this bibliography.

Andraschke, Peter. *Gustav Mahlers IX. Symphonie. Kompositions-prozess und Analyse.* Supplementary volume to the *Archiv für Musikwissenschaft,* 14. Wiesbaden, 1976.

'Struktur und Gehalt im ersten Satz von Gustav Mahlers Sechster Symphonie', *Archiv für Musikwissenschaft,* 35 (1978), 275-96.

Antonicek, Theophil. Review of the German edition of *Gustav Mahler und Guido Adler,* in *Musicologica Austriaca,* 2 (1979), 159-63.

Bahr, Hermann. 'Mahler als Direktor', *Musikblätter des Anbruch,* 2 (1920), 275-6.

Bahr-Mildenburg, Anna. 'Aus Briefen Mahlers', *Moderne Welt,* 3, 7 (1921-2), 13-14.

Erinnerungen. Vienna, 1921.

Banks, Paul. 'The Early Social and Musical Environment of Gustav Mahler'. Doctoral dissertation. University of Oxford, 1979.

'An Early Symphonic Prelude by Mahler?', *19th Century Music,* 3 (1979), 141-9.

[Bauer-Lechner, Natalie]. 'Aus einem Tagebuch über Mahler', *Der Merker,* 3 (1912), 184-8.

Erinnerungen an Gustav Mahler. Leipzig, 1923. Trans. by Dika Newlin as *Recollections of Gustav Mahler,* ed. and annotated by Peter Franklin. London, 1980. Additional portions of the previously un-published sections of Bauer-Lechner's diary are included in the work of C. Floros cited below, vol. 1, pp. 190-201.

'Mahler-Aussprüche', *Musikblätter des Anbruch,* 2 (1920), 307-9.

Bekker, Paul. *Mahlers Sinfonien.* Berlin, 1921. Reprint, Tutzing, 1969.

Bergquist, Peter. 'The First Movement of Mahler's Tenth Symphony. An

Analysis and an Examination of the Sketches', *Music Forum,* 5 (1980), 335-94.

Bernet-Kempers, Karel Philippus. 'Mahler und Willem Mengelberg', in E. Schenk (ed.), *Bericht über den Internationalen Musikwissenschaftlichen Kongress Wien Mozartjahr 1956.* Graz, 1958, pp. 41-6.

Bienenfeld, Elsa. 'Guido Adler', *Die Musik,* 18, 2 (November 1925), 113-28.

'Mahler, der Dirigent', *Moderne Welt,* 3, 7 (1921-2), 6-7.

Blaukopf, Herta. 'Als Mahlers Zeit noch nicht gekommen war', *Österreichische Musikzeitschrift,* 34 (1979), 294-7.

'Eine Oper "Aus Weber"', *Österreichische Musikzeitschrift,* 33 (1978), 204-8.

Blaukopf, Kurt. *Gustav Mahler.* Vienna, 1969. English translation by Inge Goodwin. New York, 1973.

'Gustav Mahler und die Tschechische Oper', *Österreichische Musikzeitschrift,* 34 (1979), 285-8.

(with contributions by Zoltan Roman). *Mahler. Sein Leben, sein Werk und seine Welt in zeitgenössischen Bildern und Texten.* Vienna, 1976. English translation by P. Baker, S. Flatauer, P.R.J. Ford, D. Loman and G. Watkins, as *Mahler: A Documentary Study.* London, 1976.

Brecher, Gustav. *Oberon . . . Neue Bühneneinrichtung von Gustav Mahler . . . Neue Übertragung des gesungenen Textes nach dem englischen Original sowie Vorbemerkung von Gustav Brecher.* Vienna, 1914.

Brod, Max. 'Gustav Mahlers jüdische Melodien', *Musikblätter des Anbruch,* 2 (1920), 378-9.

Bülow, Hans Guido von. *Briefe und Schriften,* ed. Marie von Bülow. 8 vols. Leipzig, 1895-1908.

Letters, ed. Richard Count de Moulin Eckart. Trans. Scott Goddard. New York, 1931. Reprint, New York, 1972.

Cardus, Neville. *Gustav Mahler: His Mind and His Music.* Vol. 1. London, 1965.

Carner, Mosco. *Of Men and Music.* London, 1944. Includes the following articles on Adler and Mahler, previously published in various periodicals: 'A Pioneer of Musicology. Guido Adler'; 'Mahler in His Letters: a Psychological Study'; 'Mahler's Visit to London'; 'Form and Technique of Mahler's "Song of the Earth" '; 'Mahler's Rescoring of the Schumann Symphonies'.

Casella, Alfredo. 'Gustav Mahler et sa deuxième Symphonie', *S. I. M. Revue musicale mensuelle,* 6 (1910), 238-50.

Chord and Discord. New York, 1932-   . Index to vol. 1 in vol. 2, 5 (1948); to vol. 2 in vol. 3, 1 (1969).

Christy, Nicholas P., Christy, Beverly M. and Wood, Barry G. 'Gustav Mahler and His Illnesses', *Transactions of the American Clinical & Climatological Association,* 82 (1970), 200-17.

Cooke, Deryck. 'The Facts Concerning Mahler's Tenth Symphony', *Chord and Discord*, 2, 10 (1963), 3-27.

Gustav Mahler (1860-1911). London, 1960. New ed., as *Gustav Mahler, An Introduction to His Music*, ed. Colin and David Matthews. London, 1980.

Decsey, Ernst. 'Stunden mit Mahler', *Die Musik*, 10, 18 (June 1911), 352-6, and 10, 21 (August 1911), 143-53.

Del Mar, Norman. *Mahler's Sixth Symphony – A Study*. London, 1980.

Diether, Jack. 'Mahler's *Klagende Lied* – Genesis and Evolution', *The Music Review*, 29 (1968), 268-87.

'Notes on Some Mahler Juvenilia', *Chord and Discord*, 3, 1 (1969), 3-100.

Dorfmüller, Kurt. 'Gustav-Mahler-Dokumente in München', *Fontes artis musicae*, 13 (1966), 33-9.

Engel, Carl. 'Guido Adler in Retrospect (1855-1941)', *The Musical Quarterly*, 27 (1941), 391-400.

Engel, Gabriel. *Gustav Mahler, Song Symphonist*. New York, 1932. Reprint, New York, 1970.

Feder, Stuart. 'Gustav Mahler um Mitternacht', *International Review of Psychoanalysis*, 7, 11 (1980), 11-26.

Filler, Susan M. 'Editorial Problems in Symphonies of Gustav Mahler: a Study of the Sources of the Third and Tenth Symphonies'. Doctoral dissertation. Northwestern University, 1977.

Floros, Constantin. *Gustav Mahler*. Vol. 1: 'Die geistige Welt Gustav Mahlers in systematischer Darstellung'. Vol. 2: 'Mahler und die Symphonie des 19. Jahrhunderts in neuer Deutung'. Wiesbaden, 1977.

Foerster, Josef Bohuslav. 'Erinnerungen an Gustav Mahler', *Musikblätter des Anbruch*, 2 (1920), 291-5.

Der Pilger: Erinnerungen eines Musikers. Prague, 1955.

Franklin, Peter. '"Funeral Rites" – Mahler and Mickiewicz', *Music & Letters*, 55 (1974), 203-8.

'The Gestation of Mahler's Third Symphony', *Music & Letters*, 58 (1977), 439-46.

Fried, Oskar. 'Erinnerungen an Mahler', *Musikblätter des Anbruch*, 1 (1919), 16-18.

Gartenberg, Egon. *Mahler: the Man and His Work*. New York, 1978.

Göhler, Georg. 'Gustav Mahlers Lieder', *Die Musik*, 10, 18 (June 1911), 357-63.

Graf, Max. 'Bruno Walter und Gustav Mahler', *Österreichische Musikzeitschrift*, 3 (1948), 100-3.

Grant, Parks. 'Bruckner and Mahler – the Fundamental Dissimilarity of Their Styles', *The Music Review*, 32 (1971), 36-55.

Gutheil-Schoder, Marie. *Erlebtes und Erstrebtes, Rolle und Gestaltung*. Vienna, 1937.

'Mahler bei der Arbeit', *Der Merker*, 3 (1912), 165.

148   *Bibliography*

'Mahleriana', *Moderne Welt*, 3, 7 (1921-2), 14-15.

Gutman, Hanns. 'Der banale Mahler', *Anbruch*, 12 (1930), 102-5.

Gutmann, Emil. 'Gustav Mahler als Organisator', *Die Musik*, 10, 18 (June 1911), 364-8.

Hadamowsky, Franz (ed.) *Ausstellung: Gustav Mahler und seine Zeit. Katalog.* Vienna, 1960.

Hartmann, Ludwig. *Opernführer. Die drei Pintos.* Leipzig, n.d. [1901].

Hirschfeld, Ludwig. '"Walküre"-Abend unter Mahler', *Moderne Welt*, 3, 7 (1921-2) 25-6. An excerpt from Hirschfeld's novella *Jupiter in der Wolke* (Berlin, 1906).

Hoffmann, Rudolph Stephan. 'Representative Wiener Mahler-Aufführungen', *Musikblätter des Anbruch*, 2 (1920), 310-12.

'Unbekannte Jugendlieder Mahlers', *Die Musikwelt* (Hamburg), 2, 2. Date and page nos. unavailable. Proof pages in Adler Collection.

Holländer, Hans. 'Gustav Mahler', *The Musical Quarterly*, 17 (1931), 449-63.

'Gustav Mahler – ein tragisches Künstlerschicksal', *Der Auftakt*, 16 (1936), 82-6.

'Gustav Mahler vollendet eine Oper von Carl Maria von Weber. Vier unbekannte Briefe Mahlers', *Neue Zeitschrift für Musik*, 116 (December 1955), 130-2.

'Neue Beiträge zu den frühen Lehrjahren Gustav Mahlers', *Schweizerische Musikzeitung*, 70 (1930), 559-62.

'Unbekannte Jugendbriefe Gustav Mahlers', *Die Musik*, 20, 11 (August 1928), 807-13.

'Ein unbekannter Teil von Gustav Mahlers "Klagendem Lied" ', *Der Auftakt*, 14, 11-12 (1934), 200-2.

Huneker, James Gibbons. *The Philharmonic Society of New York and Its Seventy-Fifth Anniversary: A Retrospect.* New York, 1917.

Jemnitz, Alexander. 'Gustav Mahler als kgl. ung. Hofoperndirektor', *Der Auftakt*, 16 (1936), 7-11, 63-7, 183-8.

Jokl, Ernst. 'Gustav Mahler in Amerika', *Musikblätter des Anbruch*, 2 (1920), 289-91.

Karpath, Ludwig. *Begegnung mit dem Genius.* Vienna, 1934.

'Gustav Mahler in Amerika', *Moderne Welt*, 3, 7 (1921-2), 33-5.

Kauder, Hugo. 'Mahlers Instrumentation', *Musikblätter des Anbruch*, 2 (1920), 277-8.

'Vom Geiste der Mahlerschen Musik', *Musikblätter des Anbruch*, 2 (1920), 262-5.

Keller, Otto. 'Gustav Mahler-Literatur', *Die Musik*, 10, 18 (June 1911), 369-77. Amplified by Arthur Seidl in *Die Musik*, 10, 21 (August 1911), 154-8.

Kennedy, Michael. *Mahler.* The Master Musicians Series. London, 1974.

Kienzl, Wilhelm. *Meine Lebenswanderung. Erlebtes und Erlauschtes.* Stuttgart, 1926.

Klein, Rudolf (ed.). *Das Wiener Gustav-Mahler-Kolloquium (11-16*

Juni 1979). Forthcoming.

Klemperer, Otto. *Erinnerungen an Gustav Mahler.* Zürich, 1960. English translation by J. Maxwell Brownjohn as part of the volume *Minor Recollections.* London, 1964, pp. 9-40.

Klusen, Ernst. 'Gustav Mahler und das Volkslied seiner Heimat', *Journal of the International Folk Music Council,* 15 (June 1963), 29-37.

Kralik, Heinrich. *Gustav Mahler.* Vienna, 1968.

Kravitt, Edward F. 'Mahler's Dirges for His Death: February 24, 1901', *The Musical Quarterly,* 64 (1978), 329-53.

Křenek, Ernst. *See* Bruno Walter, *Gustav Mahler.*

Kurz, Selma. 'Mein Entdecker', *Moderne Welt,* 3, 7 (1921-2), 15.

La Grange, Henry-Louis de. *Mahler.* Vol. 1. Garden City, New York, 1973. French edition, incorporating some revisions, *Gustav Mahler: Chronique d'une vie,* vol. 1: '1860-1900'. Paris, 1979.

    'Mahler: a New Image', *Saturday Review* (29 March 1969), 47-9, 57-8.

    'Mistakes about Mahler', *Music and Musicians,* 21, 2 (October 1972), 16-22.

Lindner, Dolf. 'Zur Ausstellung "Gustav Mahler und seine Zeit" ', *Österreichische Musikzeitschrift,* 15 (1960), 311-14.

Lipiner, Siegfried. *Der entfesselte Prometheus.* Leipzig, 1876.

    Über die Elemente einer Erneuerung religiöser Ideen in der Gegenwart. Vienna, 1878.

Löhr, Friedrich. 'Zwei Jugendbriefe: von Mahler und über ihn', *Musikblätter des Anbruch,* 2 (1920), 301-5.

Lustgarten, Egon. 'Mahlers lyrisches Schaffen', *Musikblätter des Anbruch,* 2 (1920), 269-72.

Mahler [Werfel], Alma Maria, in collaboration with E. B. Ashton. *And the Bridge is Love.* London, 1958. This volume is an adaptation of Frau Mahler's *Mein Leben*, subsequently published in Frankfurt in 1960.

Mahler, Alma Maria. *Gustav Mahler, Erinnerungen und Briefe.* Amsterdam, 1940. English translation by Basil Creighton as *Gustav Mahler, Memories and Letters.* London, 1946. 3rd ed. further enlarged with a new appendix and chronology by Knud Martner and Donald Mitchell and a new appendix for the 1975 American edition by Donald Mitchell. Seattle, 1975.

Mahler, Gustav. *Briefe 1879-1911.* ed. Alma Mahler, Berlin, 1924. Czech edition, with additional material and notes, ed. F. Bartoš. Prague, 1962. Russian edition, ed. I. Barsova, trans. S. Osherov. Moscow, 1964. English translation by E. Wilkins, E. Kaiser and B. Hopkins, as *Selected Letters of Gustav Mahler,* enlarged and edited with a new introduction, illustrations and notes by Knud Martner. London, 1979.

    'Ein Jugendgedicht', *Der Merker,* 3 (1912), 183.

'Ein Selbstporträt in Briefen', *Der Merker*, 3 (1912), 172-81.

Mahler, Gustav and Strauss, Richard. *Briefwechsel 1888-1911*. Edited, with an essay, by Herta Blaukopf. Bibliothek der Internationalen Gustav Mahler Gesellschaft. Munich, 1980.

Mahler Feestboek (May 6-21, 1920). Amsterdam, 1920.

Martner, Knud and Robert Becqué. 'Zwölf unbekannte Briefe Gustav Mahlers an Ludwig Strecker', *Archiv für Musikwissenschaft*, 34 (1977), 287-97.

Matthews, Colin. 'Mahler at Work. Aspects of the Creative Process'. Doctoral dissertation. University of Sussex, 1977.

'Mahler at Work: Some Observations on the Ninth and Tenth Symphony Sketches', *Soundings*, 4 (1974), 76-86.

McGrath, William J. *Dionysian Art and Populist Politics in Austria*. New Haven, 1974.

Mengelberg, C. Rudolf (ed.). *Das Mahler-Fest, Amsterdam, Mai 1920: Vorträge und Berichte*. Vienna, 1920.

Über den Stand der Mahler-Pflege', *Moderne Welt*, 3, 7 (1921-2), 30-1.

Der Merker. Mahler issue. 3, 5 (March 1912). Individual articles are listed separately by author in this bibliography.

Milburn, Jr, Frank. 'Mahler's Four Last Winters, Spent in New York, Are Viewed Through the Eyes of the Press', *Musical America*, 80, 3 (February 1960), 12, 164, 166, 168.

Mitchell, Donald. *Gustav Mahler, The Early Years*. London, 1958. New edition, revised and edited by Paul Banks and David Matthews. London, 1980.

Gustav Mahler, The Wunderhorn Years. London, 1975. Supplement, doctoral dissertation. University of Southampton, 1977.

'Mahler's Waldmärchen', *Musical Times*, 111 (1970), 375-9.

Mittag, Erwin. 'Gustav Mahler als Dirigent', *Österreichische Musikzeitschrift*, 15 (1960), 294-6.

Moderne Welt. Mahler issue. 3, 7 (1921-2; no month indicated in issue). Individual articles are listed separately by author in this bibliography.

Mohácsi, Jenõ. 'Gustav Mahler in Budapest', *Moderne Welt*, 3, 7 (1921-2), 27-9.

Moldenhauer, Hans. 'Unbekannte Briefe Gustav Mahlers an Emil Hertzka', *Neue Zeitschrift für Musik*, 35 (1974), 544-9.

Morgan, Robert P. 'Ives and Mahler: Mutual Responses at the End of an Era', *19th Century Music*, 2 (1978), 72-81.

Die Musik. Mahler issue. 10, 18 (June 1911). Individual articles are listed separately by author in this bibliography.

Musikblätter des Anbruch. See *Anbruch*.

Neitzel, Otto. 'Gustav Mahler und das Amsterdamer Concertgebouw', *Musikblätter des Anbruch*, 2 (1920), 256-62.

Nettl, Paul. 'Gustav Mahler als "Musikhistoriker"; ein bisher unveröffentlicher [*sic*] Brief des Meisters', *Musica,* 12 (1958), 592-5.

Newlin, Dika. *Bruckner, Mahler and Schönberg.* New York, 1947. Rev. ed., New York, 1978.

'The "Mahler's Brother Syndrome"': Necropsychiatry and the Artist', *The Musical Quarterly,* 66 (1980), 296-304.

'Mahler's Opera', *Opera News,* 18 March 1972, 6-7.

Nodnagel, Ernst Otto. *Gustav Mahlers Dritte Sinfonie in d-moll.* 2nd ed. Darmstadt, 1904.

Gustav Mahlers Fünfte Symphonie. Technische Analyse. Leipzig, 1905.

Gustav Mahlers Zweite Sinfonie. Charlottenburg, 1903.

Jenseits von Wagner und Liszt. Königsberg, 1902.

Nowak, Leopold. 'Die Kompositionen und Skizzen von Hans Rott in der Musiksammlung der Österreichischen Nationalbibliothek', in G. Brosche (ed.), *Franz Grasberger zum 60. Geburtstag.* Tutzing, 1975, pp. 273-340.

Österreichische Musikzeitschrift. Mahler issues. 15, 6 (June 1960), and 34, 6 (June 1979). Individual articles are listed separately by author in this bibliography.

Pamer, Fritz Egon. 'Gustav Mahlers Lieder'. Doctoral dissertation. University of Vienna, 1922. Published in abbreviated form in *Studien zur Musikwissenschaft,* 16 (1929), 116-38, and 17 (1930), 105-27.

Pfohl, Ferdinand. *Gustav Mahler, Eindrücke und Erinnerungen aus den Hamburger Jahren,* ed. Knud Martner. Hamburg, 1973.

Ratz, Erwin. 'Gustav Mahler 1860-1911', in *Die grossen Deutschen,* vol. 4. Berlin, 1956, pp. 282-91.

'Persönlichkeit und Werk. Zum 100. Geburtstag Gustav Mahlers', *Österreichische Musikzeitschrift,* 15 (1960), 282-91.

'Zum Formproblem bei Gustav Mahler, Eine Analyse des ersten Satzes der IX. Symphonie', *Die Musikforschung,* 8 (1955), 169-77.

'Zum Formproblem bei Gustav Mahler. Eine Analyse des Finales der VI. Symphonie', *Die Musikforschung,* 9 (1956), 156-71. English translation by Paul Hamburger as 'Musical Form in Gustav Mahler. An Analysis of the Finale of the Sixth Symphony', *The Music Review,* 29 (1968), 34-48.

Raynor, Henry. *Mahler.* London, 1975.

Redlich, Hans Ferdinand. *Bruckner and Mahler.* The Master Musicians. London, 1955. 2nd ed., 1963.

'Gustav Mahler. Probleme einer kritischer Gesamtausgabe', *Die Musikforschung,* 19 (1966), 278-401.

'Mahler's Enigmatic "Sixth"', in *Festschrift Otto Erich Deutsch zum 80. Geburtstag am 5. September 1963.* Kassel, 1963, pp. 250-6.

'Mahlers Wirkung in Zeit und Raum', *Anbruch,* 12 (1930), 92-6.

'Die Welt der V., VI. und VII. Sinfonie Mahlers', *Musikblätter des Anbruch,* 2 (1920), 265-8.

Reeser, Eduard. *Gustav Mahler und Holland. Briefe.* Bibliothek der

Internationalen Gustav Mahler Gesellschaft. Vienna, 1980.

Reich, Willi (ed.). *Gustav Mahler im eigenen Wort – im Worte der Freunde*. Zürich, 1958.

Reik, Theodor. *The Haunting Melody*. New York, 1953.

Reilly, Edward R. *Gustav Mahler und Guido Adler*. Trans. H. Blaukopf. Bibliothek der Internationalen Gustav Mahler Gesellschaft. Vienna, 1978.

'Die Skizzen zu Mahlers Zweiter Symphonie', *Österreichische Musik-zeitschrift*, 34 (1979), 266-85.

Revers, Peter. 'Zum Stand der Mahler-Forschung', *Österreichische Musikzeitschrift*, 34 (1979), 289-93.

Rezniček, Emil Nikolaus von. 'Erinnerungen an Gustav Mahler', *Musik-blätter des Anbruch*, 2 (1920), 298-300.

Ritter, William. 'La neuvième de Gustave [*sic*] Mahler', *S. I. M. Revue musicale mensuelle*, 8, 7-8 (July – August 1912), 41-7.

'Souvenirs sur Gustav Mahler', *Schweizerische Musikzeitung*, 101, 1 (January – February 1961), 29-39.

Roller, Alfred. *Die Bildnisse von Gustav Mahler*. Leipzig, 1922.

'Mahler und die Inszenierung', *Musikblätter des Anbruch*, 2 (1920), 272-5. The same article also appears in *Moderne Welt*, 3, 7 (1921-2), 4-5, and reproductions of several of Roller's set and costume designs appear in the same issue.

Roman, Zoltan. 'Aesthetic Symbiosis and Structural Metaphor in Mahler's *Das Lied von der Erde*', in I. Bontinck and O. Brusatti (eds.), *Festschrift Kurt Blaukopf*. Vienna, 1975, pp. 110-19.

Schaefer, Hans Joachim. 'Gustav Mahler in Kassel', *informationen*, issues of June, July/August 1975; February, April, May, June, July/August 1976; February, March, April, May 1977.

'Gustav Mahlers Wirken in Kassel', *Musica*, 14 (1960), 350-7.

Schalk, Franz. *Briefe und Betrachtungen*. Vienna, 1935.

Scharlitt, Bernard. 'Gespräch mit Mahler', *Musikblätter des Anbruch*, 2 (1920), 309-10.

Schiedermair, Ludwig. 'Gustav Mahler als Symphoniker', *Die Musik*, 1 (1901-2), 506-10, 603-8, 696-9.

Gustav Mahler. Dritte Symphonie. Leipzig, n.d.

Schmidt, Heinrich. 'Formprobleme und Entwicklungslinien in Gustav Mahlers Symphonien'. Doctoral dissertation. University of Vienna, 1929.

Schoenberg, Arnold. 'Gustav Mahler', *Der Merker*, 3 (1912), 182-3. Translated as 'Gustav Mahler: in memoriam', in L. Stein (ed.), *Style and Idea: Selected Writings of Arnold Schoenberg*. London, 1975, pp. 447-8.

'Gustav Mahler', in L. Stein (ed.), *Style and Idea*, pp. 449-72.

Schorske, Carl E. *Fin-de-siècle Vienna: Politics and Culture*. New York, 1980.

Schreiber, Wolfgang. *Gustav Mahler in Selbstzeugnissen und Bild-*

dokumenten. Rheinbeck bei Hamburg, 1971.

Schumann, Robert. *Gesammelte Schriften über Musik und Musiker,* ed. F. G. Jansen. Vol. 1. Leipzig, 1891.

Seidl, Arthur. *Moderner Geist in der deutschen Tonkunst.* Berlin, 1901.
'Zu Gustav Mahlers Gedächtnis. Eine nichtgehaltene Rede', *Der Merker,* 3 (1912), 192-5.
See also Otto Keller.

Seligmann, A. F. 'Silhouetten aus der Mahler-Zeit', *Moderne Welt,* 3, 7 (1921-2), 10-12.

Seltsam, William H. *Metropolitan Opera Annals.* New York, 1947.

Shanet, Howard. *Philharmonic: A History of New York's Orchestra.* Garden City, New York, 1975.

Slezak, Leo. 'Gustav Mahler', *Moderne Welt,* 3, 7 (1921-2), 16-17. Excerpted from Slezak's *Meine sämtlichen Werke.* Berlin, 1920.

Specht, Richard. *Gustav Mahler.* Moderne Essays. Berlin, 1905.
Gustav Mahler. Berlin, 1913. 2nd ed., 1918.
'Gustav Mahler', *Die Musik,* 10, 18 (June 1911), 335-41.
'Gustav Mahlers Gegenwart', *Moderne Welt,* 3, 7 (1921-2), 1-3.
Gustav Mahlers VIII. Symphonie: Thematische Analyse. Vienna, 1912.
'Mahler', *Der Merker,* 3 (1912), 161-5.
Mahler: I. Symphonie [also II., III., IV., in separate pamphlets], *Thematische Analyse.* Vienna, 1915-21.
'Mahlers Feinde', *Musikblatter des Anbruch,* 2 (1920), 278-87.

Stefan, Paul. *Das Grab in Wien: eine Chronik 1903-1911.* Berlin, 1913.
(ed.). *Gustav Mahler, ein Bild seiner Persönlichkeit in Widmungen.* Munich, 1910.
Gustav Mahler, eine Studie über Persönlichkeit und Werk. Munich, 1910. 2nd ed., 1913. English translation by T. E. Clark, New York, 1913.
'Gustav Mahler in der Literatur', *Moderne Welt,* 3, 7 (1921-2), 8-9.
'Gustav Mahlers Kindheit, erste Jugend und Lehrjahre', *Die Musik,* 10, 18 (June 1911), 342-51.
'Mahlers Freunde', *Musikblätter des Anbruch,* 2 (1920), 287-9.
'Mahler und das Theater', *Anbruch,* 12 (1930), 96-8.
'Richard Wagner und Mahler', *Der Merker,* 3 (1912), 189-91.

Stehmann, Gerhard. 'Gustav Mahlers Proben', *Moderne Welt,* 3, 7 (1921-2), 17-19.

Stein, Erwin. 'Mahlers Sachlichkeit', *Anbruch,* 12 (1930), 99-101.
Orpheus in New Guises. London, 1953. Contains the following articles on Mahler, the majority translations of earlier studies published in various periodicals: 'Mahler (1953)'; 'Mahler the Factual (1930)' (a translation of 'Mahlers Sachlichkeit', cited above); 'Organizing the Tempi of Mahler's Ninth Symphony (1924)'; 'Mahler's Rescorings (1927)'; 'The Unknown Last Version of Mahler's Fourth Symphony (1929)'; 'Mahler, Reger, Strauss and Schönberg (1926)'.

Steinitzer, Max. 'Erinnerungen an Gustav Mahler', *Musikblätter des*

Anbruch, 2 (1920), 296-8.

Stephan, Rudolf. 'Gedanken zu Mahler', *Österreichische Musikzeitschrift,* 34 (1979), 257-66.

Gustav Mahler. Werk und Interpretation. Autographe. Partituren. Dokumente. Eine Ausstellung ... Cologne, 1979.

Gustav Mahler II. Symphonie C-moll. Munich, 1979.

Strauss, Richard. *See* Gustav Mahler and Richard Strauss.

Teibler, Hermann. *Gustav Mahler. Symphonie No. 2 in C-moll.* Leipzig, n.d.

Teweles, Heinrich. 'Mahler in Prag', *Moderne Welt,* 3, 7 (1921-2), 32.

Tibbe, Monika. *Über die Verwendung von Liedern und Liedelementen in instrumentalen Symphoniesätzen Gustav Mahlers.* Berliner Musikwissenschaftliche Arbeiten, 1. Munich, 1971.

Tischler, Hans. 'Die Harmonik in den Werken Gustav Mahlers'. Doctoral dissertation. University of Vienna, 1937.

'Key Symbolism versus "Progressive Tonality" ', *Musicology,* 2 (1949), 383-8.

'Mahler's "Das Lied von der Erde" ', *The Music Review,* 10 (1949), 111-14.

'Mahler's Impact on the Crisis of Tonality', *The Music Review,* 12 (1951), 113-21.

'Musical Form in Gustav Mahler's Works', *Musicology,* 2 (1949), 231-42.

'The Symphonic Problem in Mahler's Works', *Chord and Discord,* 2, 3 (1941), 15-21.

Ullrich, Hermann. 'Gustav Mahler und Wien im Wandel der Zeiten', *Österreichische Musikzeitschrift,* 15 (1960), 297-302.

Vergo, Peter. *Art in Vienna 1898-1918.* London, 1975.

Vondenhoff, Bruno and Eleonore. *Gustav Mahler Dokumentation. Sammlung Eleonore Vondenhoff.* Tutzing, 1978.

Walker, Frank. *Hugo Wolf.* London, 1951. 2nd ed., 1968.

Walter, Bruno. *Briefe 1894-1962.* Frankfurt am Main, 1969.

'Gustav Mahler', in *The Universal Jewish Encyclopedia,* 7 (1942), pp. 282-4.

Gustav Mahler. Vienna, 1936. English translation by James Galston, with a biographical essay by Ernst Křenek. New York, 1941. Another translation 'supervised' by Lotte Walter Lindt. New York, 1958. Reprint of the Galston translation, New York, 1970.

'Mahlers Weg. Ein Erinnerungsblatt', *Der Merker,* 3, 5 (1912), 166-71.

Thema und Variationen. Stockholm, 1947. English translation by James Galston. New York, 1946.

Warrack, John. *Carl Maria von Weber.* New York, 1968. 2nd ed., 1976.

Weigl, Karl. *Gustav Mahler: Siebente Symphonie (E moll).* Berlin, n.d.

Weingartner, Felix. *Lebenserinnerungen.* Vienna, 1923. English translation by Marguerite Wolff, under the title *Buffets and Rewards: a Musician's Reminiscences.* London, 1937.

Weingartner-Studer, Carmen. 'Gustav Mahler und Felix Weingartner', *Österreichische Musikzeitschrift,* 15 (1960), 308-10.

Wellesz, Egon. 'Anfänge der "Neuen Musik" in Wien', *Österreichische Musikzeitschrift,* 25 (1970), 312-15.

'Mahlers Instrumentation', *Anbruch,* 12 (1930), 106-10.

'Reminiscences of Mahler', *The Score,* 28 (January 1961), 52-5.

'The Symphonies of Gustav Mahler', *The Music Review,* 1 (1940), 2-23.

'An Unpublished Letter of Mahler', *The Music Review,* 1 (1940), 24.

Wenk, Arthur B. 'The Composer as Poet in *Das Lied von der Erde',* *19th Century Music,* 1 (1977), 33-47.

Werba, Erik. 'Ein "Mahler"-Brief', *Österreichische Musikzeitschrift,* 16 (1960), 292-4.

Wessling, Berndt W. *Gustav Mahler.* Hamburg, 1974.

Wiener akademischer Wagner-Verein. Siebenter Jahres-Bericht für das Jahr 1879. Vienna, 1880.

Wiesmann, Sigrid (ed.). *Gustav Mahler in Vienna.* Translated by Anne Shelley. New York, 1976.

Wildgans, Friedrich. 'Gustav Mahler und Anton von Webern', *Österreichische Musikzeitschrift,* 15 (1960), 302-6.

Wooldridge, David. *From the Steeples and Mountains: a Study of Charles Ives.* New York, 1974.

Wöss, Josef Venantius von. *Gustav Mahler, Das Lied von der Erde: Thematische Analyse.* Vienna, 1912.

Zweig, Stefan. *The World of Yesterday.* New York, 1943. Paperback reprint, Lincoln, Nebraska, 1964.

INDEX